Radical
Hospitality

David and Ruth Rupprecht

Presbyterian and Reformed Publishing Company
Phillipsburg, New Jersey 08865

Unless otherwise indicated, all Scripture quotations are from the New
International Version, copyright © 1978 by New York International Bible
Society.

The chapter head illustration of Berachah Barn was done by Blais
Brancheau, who lived with the Rupprechts for four years.

PRINTED IN THE UNITED STATES OF AMERICA

Library of Congress Cataloging in Publication Data

Rupprecht, David, 1947-
    Radical hospitality.

    1. Hospitality—Religious aspects—Christianity.
2. Rupprecht, David, 1947-   . 3. Rupprecht,
Ruth, 1944-   I. Rupprecht, Ruth, 1944-
II. Title.
BV4647.H67R86   1983   261.8′3   83-3259
ISBN 0-87552-421-4
ISBN 0-87552-420-6 (pbk.)

For Susan
and
for Charlie

who, by unselfishly exercising diverse gifts,
have "radical-ized" our home and hospitality.

Contents

1. Virginia and the Multitude of Her Sisters and Brothers 1

2. Radical Hospitality 11

3. "And You Are to Love Those Who Are Aliens . . ." 17

4. "These People Have No Place to Go . . . " 24

5. "And There Are Varieties of Ministries . . ." ... 30

6. Self-Evaluation—The Start 43

7. Is This the One? Or Should We Look for Another? 62

8. Parents—The Other Side of the Coin 73

9. Mucking It Out 85

10. The Local Church—The Place for Help 102

11. Pray Without Ceasing—And You Will Pray! 109

Acknowledgments

Our special thanks:

to Sharon Pruden and Sue Morgan for their assistance in typing the manuscript,

to Eugene Priddy and Keynote Ministries—Bible Basics International—for the use of their word processor,

to our family and church body for their encouragement, support, and their excellent child care while we were researching and writing.

CHAPTER ONE

Virginia and the Multitude of Her Sisters and Brothers

Sometimes the only private place to talk in the barn that has become our home is a tiny bathroom tucked at the end of our downstairs hall. That was the case one cold, winter Saturday morning. Our own two children were parked in front of "Sesame Street"; Sheree, who had been with us for a month, was already at work at a local nursing home; Blais and Jeff, full-time additions to our household, were finishing breakfast; and Gunnar, a college student visiting for the weekend, was finally out of bed. This bustle of activity, even in a house as large as ours, was enough to send us scurrying to the warmth and solitude of our bathroom.

We had been opening our home to those who needed a sense of family, a place to begin anew, for about six years. About twenty people had moved in and out of our doors during that time, some having found here a place of blessing, a *berachah*, from which our barn drew its name, and others, only a stop from which they would resume their

1

path toward ultimate destruction. But on that morning we were to make a decision to "trust in the Lord and do good," that indeed would cause us to lean on the goodness of our God.

Virginia first came to our attention through a woman in our congregation who lived in the same apartment complex she did. They had become friends as they and their children waited each day for the school bus. It wasn't long before Judy's warmth and friendliness gave Virginia the assurance that she could confide in her. When Virginia began to share her extensive marital problems, Judy encouraged her to see David for counseling.

Meeting Virginia for the first time was something like discovering a scared rabbit. Extremely thin and pale, she would glance nervously around, checking to see, as it were, if she were being watched or followed. She had next to no confidence, no sense of belonging. Speaking only when spoken to, she was afraid to share her ideas with others, lest she say the wrong thing.

Virginia began seeing one of our church counselors for weekly sessions. After eight months of counseling, she became convinced that her safety and that of her son depended on their leaving her abusive husband, a man who drank heavily, never held a steady job, and spent much time maligning her. Leaving was not easy. Virginia herself had few resources—the main one, a brother and sister-in-law who grudgingly agreed to let her come with them, though only until she could get settled, the sooner the better.

The day after Christmas we received a phone call from a sobbing Virginia. Yes, she had left her husband, but he had followed her and taken their son Bobby, telling Virginia that, unless she cooperated, she would never see Bobby again. Her brother and his wife were trying to help, but no one knew what to do. So, as the New Year began, we accompanied her to Legal Aid to begin the custody process that was to reunite her and her son ten days later.

That crisis temporarily over, we were greeted one morning by another caller, voice shaking and high-pitched. "I want that woman out!" screamed Virginia's sister-in-law. "She's brought only trouble, trouble, trouble." Ruth pulled the receiver away from her ear as the woman continued to rant and rave. We had heard many bizarre descriptions of this relative, and that compounded the difficulty of putting into perspective the claims she was now making.

Virginia herself appeared troubled when she brought Bobby for his counseling session that Friday evening. The frightened look that was her trademark during the previous autumn had reappeared. Desperation again filtered through her voice as she blurted that she wanted to find an apartment but hadn't any money and feared that her husband would discover where she lived and take Bobby again.

So, when we found our bathroom hideaway that wintry morning, we both knew that our family would again be temporarily expanded and the barn walls stretched to accommodate two more who needed shelter.

Our decision was based on an unmistakable need. And yet, our human feelings of having to extend ourselves even more could not be ignored. Our own children were our first responsibility. That has always been a cardinal principle in our ministry. We had Sheree with us already, and space would be tight. Bringing an additional child into our situation would, naturally, add noise and bustle. And, for all we knew, Virginia's husband might show up one night with a gun and demand his child.

As the car bearing Virginia and her son drove in at noon, Ruth could hardly fight back the tears. Every cell in her body seemed to be aching, "We're too overwhelmed. Can't somebody else do it? Why does everyone expect us to come through?" Finding David in the garage, about to help unload the suitcases and boxes, Ruth pleaded, "Pray with me; I don't think I can take this. I know the need, but it's just too hard to have two more."

Standing in that garage, arms around each other, we asked God to give us His power and love as we welcomed our newcomers. We acknowledged our helplessness, our inability to respond apart from God's mediating grace. And we began to carry in boxes and baskets to what was once our bedroom, but would now provide a place for a troubled woman and her son.

The next day, while riding home from church, Virginia and Ruth spoke of dividing up the household chores. After some discussion, Virginia turned to Ruth. "I don't want to make you angry," she began, her voice starting to quaver, "but I may not get everything done in one day. I don't want to make you yell at me."

Ruth turned to face her, sensing more deeply the terror she must have known both in her own home and at her brother's. As Ruth gently explained that we work to understand each other rather than raise our voices, she could not help but wonder at her previous day's feelings centered on her own, lesser needs.

To say Virginia began to change in the next few weeks would be an understatement. Her initial taste of a new beginning came as she got Bobby on the school bus each morning for a week straight. Before that, her husband would allow him to stay home if he complained of the slightest pain. Bobby also began to eat healthy food rather than filling in with desserts, and he began to see that Mommy could set limits and hold to them.

At first Virginia wanted to retreat to the privacy of her

room, afraid that she was interfering in our lives. We would make it a point to include her in an after-dinner activity or a Sunday afternoon gathering. She established a routine for herself with a specific rising time, chore time, study time with Bobby and his homework, and bedtime. Later, she was to tell us that for the first time in her life she felt as if she could do things right. Gradually, her fear of rejection and being an added burden dissipated, and she started to relax.

A call from her lawyer one Thursday in March almost erased all of the progress she had been making. Her husband's family had filed counter-charges against her, and her brother and sister-in-law had also turned against her. A court-appointed psychologist, who had seen her only briefly, had recommended Bobby be given to his father. A hearing was scheduled for the next Friday, and practically all hope vanished.

On Virginia's side of the case were Bobby's improved school record and the positive reports of the state child welfare worker, but time seemed against her, and she was totally dismayed. We, who had spoken to her so often of God's care and concern, spoke reassuringly to her again, bolstering our own faltering faith at the same time. Feverishly we tried to gather evidence to show that she was parenting well, as we prayed all the while for God's intervention.

Intervention came first in the form of a postponement of the custody hearing for two weeks. Virginia sobbed with relief at the news of the postponement, "I knew I had to trust God. I wish I could trust Him more." So, again we gathered our facts, conferred with her caring lawyer, and prayed with our entire church.

The night before we were to go to court, Ruth sat upstairs in our living room reading Psalm 37. "Trust in the Lord and do good. . . . The wicked draw the sword and bend the bow to bring down the poor and needy. . . . But their swords will pierce their own hearts. . . . the Lord will not leave them [the righteous] in their power or let them be condemned when brought to trial."

Virginia climbed the steps after Bobby had fallen asleep, and we sat down to tea. "You must be sorry that you ever got involved with me," she began. "I'm really a lot of trouble to you and your husband."

Ruth's mind went back to that Saturday when she first came, and those feelings of being overwhelmed. We had since discussed with Virginia how Ruth sometimes did feel exhausted and wearied, but that God had so often provided others to bring relief and His grace to bear her share.

Ruth's mind returned to Psalm 37. "No, I'm not sorry," she answered. "I've just been reading that we are to trust the Lord and do good, and no matter what happens tomorrow, we are sure that what we've done is good, and we certainly have trusted in the Lord." We read the rest of the Psalm together, and we all slept well despite any misgivings about the next day.

As we sat in the narrow hallway between courtrooms, waiting for Virginia's lawyer to appear, we felt strangely relaxed. The six of us—Virginia, her therapist, two church friends, and we—watched the time pass slowly as another case dragged on before hers could even be heard.

The elevator opened with what must have been its twentieth motion of the morning, but this time Virginia's lawyer, the child welfare worker, and the court-appointed psychologist who had done the evaluation strode swiftly past. Mark, the lawyer, escorted the others inside the judge's chamber and returned to us.

"Are you still praying?" was the first question he asked Virginia. She nodded. "Well, Dr. Simpson has changed his mind, and he is recommending to the judge that custody remain with you." There was an explosion of joy and gratitude, bringing out the bailiff from another courtroom where a criminal trial was proceeding.

That day we left the court with a continuation of the temporary order giving custody to Virginia until further testing could be done. Soon after that Virginia committed her life to Christ, having realized that He cared for her and had overcome so many obstacles.

God still had many more lessons to teach us. Bobby started to see his father more, and his dad used the visits to try to turn him against Virginia. Time and again after Bobby returned from such a session, Virginia would listen to him tell her of how she had beaten him as a baby and left him many times, all of which were falsehoods.

Rather than counter with stories of her own, Virginia channeled her energy toward others. She spent afternoons with a friend dying of cancer, improved her sewing, and was on her way to being independent enough to meet others' needs. She had learned to get along with many different kinds of people, with all the traffic passing in and out of our doors each week. She handled without complaint her end of our daily chores and all the dishes that piled in our sink.

Summer found us settled somewhat comfortably into our pattern. Virginia had the goal of finding a job and moving out on her own at the end of the next school year. Another telephone call from her lawyer again upset her plans.

The reports had come back from the psychiatrist, and this time the judge would make a final settlement of the custody question. As we approached the court date, we were even more confident, since Virginia had passed the psychiatric evaluation, and all the reports from the state and county agencies involved were positive toward custody remaining with her.

The surprise came when the lawyers conferenced the case that Friday, and the judge announced he was for joint custody. Virginia was stunned and would not agree to have her son spend half of his time back in the situation she had so struggled to escape. The judge begrudgingly set a date for the hearing to begin, but warned he was going on vacation and wanted the case over.

The night before the hearing we again met with her lawyer to go over testimony. The mood was anything but hopeful, since our State Supreme Court had just published the findings of its investigative commission, which was recommending joint custody in nearly every custody case. Yet we prayed and knew that God is sovereign and His ways are often higher than ours.

The first day of the proceedings, about two hours into the testimony of the child welfare worker, Janet, the judge suddenly became ill and the hearing was postponed. The next day the judge was still ill. Thursday the case had a late start because Virginia's husband's attorney was confused as to when the hearing would again begin. By the end of Thursday, Janet was still being cross-examined, and it seemed the proceedings would never end.

That weekend we continued to pray. We knew God had intervened, but we weren't sure for what purpose. Virginia's lawyer began to press her to settle out of court. After prayer, this seemed the best thing to do—to draw up terms favorable to her and see what the judge would rule.

Tuesday was another long day outside the courtroom doors. Mark and Janet, with our plan in hand, joined the other lawyer before the judge. Virginia and Ruth remained in the waiting room, reading, pacing, and praying. She asked Ruth to evaluate her growth as a Christian. We discussed the new dimension of trust in God she would learn if Bobby were given more into the hands of his father. She spoke of being ready to do that.

An hour later Mark and Janet came back with unbelievable smiles. The judge had presented his plan, which incredibly matched the one we had drawn up, with one remarkable exception: he was recommending sole custody for Virginia, giving her decision-making powers! Now all that was necessary was for both Virginia and her husband to agree. She consented readily, even though it meant that her husband would have more time with Bobby than before.

The waiting seemed endless for Virginia's husband to make his decision. Our prayers for God's continued intervention remained fervid. Two hours later, his lawyer motioned to Mark, who joyfully announced to us that Virginia's husband was willing to settle.

The extent of God's working seemed unreal as we returned to the courtroom and heard the judge so order what had been worked out on paper. It had not yet sunk in, even by the time we picked up our children from the babysitter, and we all sang at Virginia's request,

> Sing praises to God, sing praises,
> Sing praises to God, sing praises,
> For He is the King of all the earth
> Sing praises to His name.

But as we called the good news through our church prayer chain, it finally did hit home: God had intervened to give more than we could have asked or hoped.

We spoke later that week with Virginia's lawyer, who by now had become a good friend. Mark reviewed for us his initial contact with Virginia and the case and how he had thought in many ways her situation was hopeless.

"She wouldn't have made it without you," he concluded. "This woman had nothing—no money, no family, no real place to live. It's incredible how this turned out. One of the best child welfare workers was assigned to the case; Virginia saw an excellent therapist; she found some real friends; and all this just in the past eight months. Back in January I was sure she'd completely fall apart any minute, and now she is on her way to being confident."

Virginia is not the same today as she was that cold winter morning. She smiles when you first greet her, she initiates conversation, and she openly shares of what God has done. Even those in our church who do not know her well speak of the changes. She, like the rest of us, has a long journey ahead. Yet her trust and confidence in God have grown, and she wants them to continue to grow.

Our home in many ways has been a gift. A family member gave us the money that covered its initial small purchase price when it was still a cow barn. Many hands helped transform it into a people-dwelling. God has called us as husband and wife to live in harmony with each other. Our church and physical families have given much emotional and prayer support.

To draw our walls around us would be selfish and sinful, while to open to those outside who need to come in is to know firsthand the transforming power of Christ. It is an overwhelming task, and feelings at times run highly negative. Yet opening our home to Virginia has been just one witness to the truth of I Thessalonians 5:11: "The one who calls you is faithful and He will do it."

CHAPTER TWO

Radical Hospitality

We've found that the vast majority of people don't need a professional psychiatrist. They need, first of all, someone to listen to them, someone to love them, and something to feel a part of, a family in particular. This is usually ninety percent of the problem (George O'Carroll).

God sets the lonely in families (Ps. 68:6).

We all are surrounded by broken, bruised, and battered fellow humans. Examples quickly multiply. Sociologists and psychologists accumulate statistics of broken families, bruised lives, and battered children, all of which are borne out by the Virginias with whom we cross paths every day.

What is to be the response of the Christian church to these? Certainly we affirm that the gospel of Christ alone can redeem. We have been given the ministry of reconciliation to present the message that if anyone is in Christ, he is a new creation; the old is passing, the new is coming! (II Cor.

11

5:17-19). Yet, the question remains: How can this message of good news and hope reach those who are overwhelmed and crushed?

The family is God's oldest institution, established at creation when God saw that it was not good for man to be alone. Eve, with whom Adam could have communication, was created to be his suitable helper. Together they were to have dominion over creation and increase in number. Although their disobedience to God wrought strain and alienation in their relationship, He did not rescind the family structure itself. Adam and Eve would face the new tensions of sin in marriage after the fall, by God's mercy alone.

Christian marriage, with its product, the Christian home, is to be the model of the relationship between Christ and His church, according to Ephesians 5. When the church is in proper relationship, both to those within it and to Christ Himself, the world may know that Jesus Christ is God and be drawn to Him. Likewise, the Christian family, with marriage partners made a new creation through the reconciling work of Christ and living in right biblical relationship to each other, is a demonstration to the world that obedience to God brings with it practical, everyday benefits of wholeness. Broken lives need to see this model of wholeness if they are to have hope of re-creation and respond to the good news of the gospel.

In recent years, Christians have been reminded of their basic ministry of hospitality. *Open Heart, Open Home,* by Karen Mains, and *Be My Guest,* by Virginia Hall, both have emphasized our duty as believers to use our homes for others. The New Testament writers, Paul, Peter, and John, challenged the early church toward this end.

Paul told the believers at Rome, "Share with God's people who are in need. Practice hospitality" (Rom. 12:13). Peter charged his readers to "offer hospitality to one another without grumbling" (I Pet. 4:9). The apostle John in III John 8 affirms that "we ought therefore to show hospitality."

Although a typical dictionary definition limits hospitality to "friendly and generous entertainment of guests," the underlying meaning is that of making these guests feel at ease, making them feel so welcome as to be a part of the whole. Hospitality, as has been so aptly defined by Karen Mains, emphasizes not the host or hostess but the guest; not what I have, but what you share with me! Its concern is not what you think of me, or how I impress you. It is other-centered, and it brings a sense of relief and life as it contrasts with the coldness of the everyday, competitive world.

Opening our homes to friends and others with whom we hold much in common brings great enjoyment to most of us. A good meal and shared laughter give a sense of warmth and acceptance. Yet Jesus, having been invited to the home of a Pharisee, had words of admonition for him and for us:

> When you give a luncheon or dinner, do not invite your friends, your brothers or relatives, or your rich neighbors; if you do, they may invite you back and so you will be repaid. But when you give a banquet, invite the poor, the crippled, the lame, the blind, and you will be blessed. Although they cannot repay you, you will be repaid at the resurrection of the righteous (Luke 14: 12-14).

Radical hospitality obeys this command. While we often think of radical as being extreme, its primary meaning is "going to the center, foundation, or source of something; fundamental; basic." Radical hospitality says to the disheartened individual, "Stay with us, see us as we really are. We'll love you, we'll deal with you, we'll stick with you, and we'll encourage you to become all that God intended you to become. By God's grace, we will not give up."

The ministry of radical hospitality is basic, though it is often not easy. It is opening a Christian home—a home where family members are consciously working at their relationships to the Lord God and to each other—to someone who has been torn emotionally or relationally by sin or by others, so that he or she can see firsthand the power of God to redeem, change, and heal. It is bringing the Virginias and her multitude of sisters and brothers into a place of refuge where somebody will listen, will love, will accept. It is bringing them into a place of challenge where God's law is the standard for behavior, where sin is defined, where manipulation is thwarted. It is what the psalmist cherished when he wrote, "God sets the lonely in families" (Ps. 68:6).

Radical hospitality has three components for the most effective ministry to occur:

1. Mature, stable Christian families are needed to be the expediters of God's healing. They must model the principles found in Scripture of imitating Christ, acting both with His authority and with His servant mentality. They must become emissaries of love and discipline so as to move the newcomer toward a life restructured upon spiritual and emotional healing. Such families must not fear that their weaknesses will surface and be seen; they do not present a model of perfection, but rather of "being confident of this, that he who began a good work in you will carry it on to completion until the day of Jesus Christ" (Phil. 1:6).

When people first learn of our ministry, they often react by saying, "You must be very special people." It is not that way at all. We have the same frustration level and needs as others. At times our calling has not brought with it immediate acceptance of a certain individual. The discouragements are many. Such a ministry could never succeed on the basis of one's own specialness.

Radical hospitality is the work of the Holy Spirit. Its success depends on the fruit of the Spirit coming to expression in the life of the believer—that fruit of love, joy, peace, patience, kindness, goodness, faithfulness, gentleness, and self-control. Where such fruit is evident in one's life, it reflects not one's inherent, extraordinary character, but God's grace.

2. The second component in radical hospitality is the support of the local church body, as partners with a ministering family. While the family is God's oldest institution, the Christian home is seen in Ephesians 5 as the microcosm of the church; it belongs under the authority of the larger unit. Thus, radical hospitality is a ministry of the local church. It is carried out in submission to the church body, which provides needed assistance through prayer and physical relief in the battle against spiritual principalities and powers. By affording supervision and aid in decision making, the church guards the family from becoming an authoritarian and dictatorial structure in its own right. The family thereby learns Spirit-filled submission to a higher authority and benefits from the many advisors and counselors of which the Old Testament proverbs often speak.

Virginia flourished in our home not only because we provided a place of refuge, but because others in our church became her close friends and supporters. She knew there were other homes where she was welcome for an afternoon cup of tea or some sewing advice. Others invited her and her son for dinner, making them special in themselves and not just a part of us. The importance of partnership between ministering family and supportive local church ought not be underestimated.

3. The final component in radical hospitality, as we are defining it, has to do with the recipient of such hospitality,

the bruised reed or dimly burning wick of which Isaiah speaks. This individual may have serious emotional or personality problems. He or she may have been alienated by shattered family relationships. He may need a new beginning, another chance. He may be an orphan. He may be an elderly person with nowhere else to turn. There are many variables, but the need is constant: such a person needs the healing touch of Jesus Christ. For some, there must be initial salvation; for others, the continued bearing of one another's burdens, so that each may eventually bear his own. Radical hospitality provides a time of refuge and works toward the goal of reuniting the bruised individual with his family or providing the means for him to find a new independence.

Finding people in need is not difficult. Within every church there are some who long for this type of healing. By caring for them, the Christian community demonstrates to an uncaring world God's concern for the alien and stranger. It is not an easy task; it is not one in which visible results come quickly. If, however, each local congregation would develop three or four such ministering families, the church would be well on its way to accomplishing a ministry of reconciliation, inviting those rejected by the world to become the righteousness of God (II Cor. 5:21).

CHAPTER THREE

"And You Are to Love Those Who Are Aliens . . ."

Each day we are bombarded with overt reminders of the vastness of human need. Our televisions flash stories of bag women in our cities. The plight of the mentally handicapped in our institutions finds sympathetic reporters seeking exposé after exposé. *National Geographic* reminds us that there is outright starvation in the refugee camps in Africa. Local newspapers focus on the family hit by tragedy. We find ourselves overwhelmed by the immensity of the woe or indifferent due to overexposure.

As Christians, we declare that we order our lives based on God's revelation in the Scripture, rather than merely emotional response. Need alone, no matter how dire it is, is not sufficient to bring the Christian into action. Whether we should act, and how, depends on God's assessment of a situation, and He does not leave us without His thoughts, especially in the area of ministering to the alien and the stranger through radical hospitality.

Deuteronomy 10:19 commands, "And you are to love those who are aliens. . . ." When we have examined who this alien is and how we are to show him love, we can gauge our involvement, or lack of involvement, in the needs of the world, with God's standard as the yardstick.

The alien, as defined in the Old Testament, was one who was passing through another's land. The stranger, or sojourner, was a resident alien living in the foreign land as opposed to traveling through. Both found themselves in a place of disadvantage. They were often unable to secure food on their own in an agricultural society, where land was needed to grow one's own produce. They were in danger of being used and manipulated by the natives of a region, who knew the language, customs, and system of government better than they. In effect, the alien and the stranger were weak and powerless, and dependent on others for refuge, protection, and provision.

Israel, God's people, was at times herself in the place of the alien, as Deuteronomy 10:19 comments: ". . . for you yourselves were aliens in Egypt." During a time of famine, Jacob and his sons made their way to Egypt, where their son and brother Joseph had been placed in a high government position. There the Israelites were given food, shelter, and protection until a new king, who did not know about Joseph, came into power. Suddenly the people of God were oppressed as aliens. Though they were politically powerless, Pharaoh feared the sheer volume of their population and therefore ordered the murder of all male newborns.

After the exodus from Egypt, Israel again found herself in the role of alien as she journeyed toward the Promised Land. At times Israelites were allowed to pass freely through the territory of another king, but often they were subjected to mockery, assault, and attack, although God Himself became their defense, causing the nations around them to be filled with dread. By the time Israel entered the Promised Land, she knew only too well how it felt to be the alien and the stranger.

Years later, as King David led his people in prayer before God after the gifts had been given for the temple, he acknowledged another level of alien status. David confessed to Jehovah, on behalf of the nation, "We are aliens and strangers in your sight, as were all our forefathers. Our days on earth are like a shadow, without hope." The only hope David saw of changing this status was found in God Himself. "I know, my God, that you test the heart and are pleased with integrity. . . . O Lord, God of our Fathers Abraham, Isaac and Israel, keep this desire in the hearts of your people forever, and keep their hearts loyal to you" (I Chron. 29:15, 17a, 18).

In the New Testament, the apostle Paul uses the concept of alien and stranger to show the Ephesian Christians what they were before they were adopted into the family of God through salvation in Christ Jesus. Paul reminds them, "Consequently, you are no longer foreigners and aliens, but fellow citizens with God's people and members of God's household" (Eph. 2:19).

The apostle Peter emphasizes that, as Christians, we are not yet beyond the alien and stranger status, but here the concept of alien and stranger has a positive meaning. After stating that we who were once not a people are now the people of God, he urges, ". . . as aliens and strangers in the world, abstain from sinful desires, which war against your soul." The Christian, then, like the Old Testament Israelite, is one who can love the alien, because he himself knows what it was to be an alien to God and is now an alien in the world.

When King David confessed before the Lord that Israel indeed was a people of aliens and strangers, he also acknowledged that it was Jehovah Himself who had been their heavenly host. David spoke both of God's greatness, splendor, power, and majesty, and of how this great magnificent God had compassion on His people. "Everything comes from you, and we have given you only what comes from your hand," David declares in I Chronicles 29:14b. The shepherd-turned-king expresses the same idea with a different metaphor in Psalm 23, when he asserts, "You prepare a table before me in the presence of my enemies" (Ps. 23:5).

Isaiah further portrays God as the heavenly host when he says in Isaiah 25:6, "On this mountain the Lord Almighty will prepare a feast of rich foods for all peoples, a banquet of aged wine—the best of meats and the finest of wines." In the final book of the New Testament, the apostle John also envisions God as the host for the wedding supper of the Lamb. All of God's care and hospitality to His people may be summed up in the promise found in I Peter 5:7: "Cast all your anxiety on him because He cares for you."

God's people, then, are called to be imitators of Him. We have been the recipients of God's grace and care. In turn, we are to act as God Himself would mercifully act toward those who are still aliens and strangers.

God gave specific commands to Old Testament Israel regarding everyday treatment of the alien and stranger. In the law of Moses, Israel was twice told not to mistreat the alien or oppress him (Exod. 22:21; 23:9). Harvesters were charged not to gather every last item of produce but to leave some for the poor and alien to glean for food (Lev. 19:9, 10). God is pictured in Deuteronomy 10:18 as loving the alien, giving him food and clothing. His people, then, were to meet these needs as well.

Isaiah again gives a summary of what God requires of those who wish to worship Him. In a passage where Israel is portrayed as having fasted and humbled herself, all without God seeming to have noticed, Isaiah speaks God's mind to the people:

> Is not this the kind of fasting I have chosen:
> to loose the chains of injustice
>   and untie the cords of the yoke,
> to set the oppressed free
>   and break every yoke?
> Is it not to share your food with the hungry
>   and to provide the poor wanderer with shelter—
> when you see the naked, to clothe him
>   and not to turn away from your own flesh and blood?
> Then your light will break forth like the dawn,
>   and your healing will quickly appear;
> then your righteousness will go before you,
>   and the glory of the Lord will be your rear guard.
> Then you will call, and the Lord will answer;
>   you will cry for help and he will say: Here am I.
>
> (Isa. 58:5-9)

Jesus Christ commanded His disciples, in like fashion, to meet the needs of those without. He announced that when the Son of Man came in glory, He would say to those on His right,

> "Come, you who are blessed by my Father, take your inheritance, the kingdom prepared for you since the creation of the world. For I was hungry and you gave me something to eat. I was thirsty and you gave me something to drink, I was a stranger and you invited me in, I needed clothes and you clothed me, I was sick and you looked after me, I was in prison and you visited me."
>
> Then the righteous will answer him, "Lord, when did we see you hungry and feed you, or thirsty and give you something to drink? When did we see you a stranger and invite you in, or needing clothes and clothe you?

When did we see you sick or in prison and go to visit you?"

The King will reply, "I tell you the truth, whatever you did for one of the least of these brothers of mine, you did for me" (Matt. 25:34-40).

Christ went on to speak of destruction for those who claimed to be ministering for Him, but failed to meet the physical needs of others around them.

In at least two other New Testament passages, the need for giving physical as well as emotional and spiritual relief is presented. James gives the challenge: "Suppose a brother or sister is without clothes and daily food. If one of you says to him, 'Go, I wish you well; keep warm and well fed,' but does nothing about his physical needs, what good is it? In the same way, faith by itself, if it is not accompanied by action, is dead" (James 2:15-17).

The apostle John in I John 3:17-18 adds this in his discussion of the nature of love. "If anyone has material possessions and sees his brother in need but has no pity on him, how can the love of God be in him? Dear children, let us not love with words or tongue but with actions and with truth."

In Old Testament Israel, the alien often came into the land because of famine or feud. God had commanded His people to meet the alien's physical needs. Often this was done as the alien became part of a priestly family who would help to provide for him. Eventually the goal was for such a one to be a proselyte in the Hebrew faith, receiving the covenant sign of circumcision. This was part of God's plan to draw those far from Him to Himself through His people, who were to be the means of blessing to all nations.

And who are our brothers in Christ? Jesus Himself gave the criterion: "For whoever does the will of my Father in heaven is my brother and sister and mother" (Matt. 12:50).

The family of God is not a closed circle, and just as Old Testament Israel was to lead the alien to be a proselyte, so our goal should be to expand the household of faith by welcoming the modern-day alien and stranger, welcoming him as a brother who has responded to the invitation of a loving Father.

CHAPTER FOUR

"These People Have No Place to Go . . ."

It is Christmas day. The wind-chill factor brings the temperature to about thirty below. Chuck and Sheree Benning are about to spend the first of three nights huddled in the laundry room of the housing project building from which they have been evicted.

When Chuck lost his job, they moved in with friends, but were told to leave by the housing authorities, who had discovered too many inhabitants in the apartment. Money has run out, and their so-called friends have little pity. State agencies are almost helpless, since their resources have long been expended. "Try Pastor Dave at Berachah Barn," the young couple is told. "He might take you."

The year 1981 marked, along with many other swings, a shift from government involvement in the life of society toward what President Reagan termed volunteerism. As New York City faced the winter of 1981–82, its Mayor Koch echoed Reagan's call with a challenge to each church and

24

synagogue within New York's five boroughs to provide
temporary housing for ten of the homeless men for whom
the city could not make provisions. "It is your Judaeo-
Christian duty," stated Koch in his appeal for help.

Elsewhere, another marriage has collapsed. The husband, ego hurting, seeks help. The world and its system
urges him to strike back, to assert himself. A Christian
family provides love and emotional care within the haven of
their home so that the hurts can be minimized as this
scarred individual sorts through the options and begins to
see healing.

In another setting, a Legal Aid lawyer stands before a
judge, defending his clients, two elderly women. They
have become a nuisance, their landlord complains. The
other tenants have been bothered by their singing late at
night. "But, Judge," their lawyer pleads, "these people
have no place to go."

Still elsewhere, a caseworker for youth and family services rushes to a home to bring a battered wife and child to
safety. The client is utterly grateful. The caseworker continues services. Three days later the wife has returned to the
scene of the abuse. She has no other resources, no one to
provide a day by day support. The caseworker's hands are
tied.

For too long, the church has given token support to the
true needs of our society. We have been content to let
government programs provide services, thus assuaging our
consciences and creating a ready target for our complaints
of waste and fraud. Recent cutbacks in these programs
leave the church with little choice; we must, as Mayor Koch
aptly asserted, perform our Judaeo-Christian duty, or allow
ourselves and our God to be scorned and ridiculed. To
paraphrase the scribes' verbal abuse of Christ, the modern-

day critic might say of us: "They saved themselves; others they would not save."

The bruised, broken and battered in our society need a new start. That is what radical hospitality affords. It is the practical ministry of warming and filling, of which James speaks, not as an end in itself, but as a means of sharing new life through Jesus Christ.

Stress has been defined by *Webster's New World Dictionary* (College Edition, 1966) as "strain, pressure; especially force that strains and deforms." Our society is menaced by the forces that strain and deform in stressful situations. Some of this stress comes about because of a person's own sinfulness; other stress is caused by the fallen environment of which we are a part. Stress often affects an individual's perception of himself, others, and his surroundings. Radical hospitality can effectively lower stress levels and clarify confused perceptions on the part of the distraught people burdened by guilt or some anxiety about the future.

As Jesus deals gently with us, though we were misguided and ignorant, we likewise ought to show compassion to those held captive by Satan's deception. That may well mean inviting people out of stressful situations that tend to compound their confusion and into a home where God's law is given due regard.

Most recipients of radical hospitality fall into that category: children who have been abused, teenagers who are rebellious, adults who have lost direction and need godly counsel. Blinded by Satan, they have no vision for what they could be in Christ, and therefore no perception of how to handle stress when it comes. Mishandled stress intensifies this blindness, causing those under its burden to settle for faulty, short-range goals. When the faulty goals do not satisfy, the stress is only intensified, and the cycle begins to spiral tighter and tighter.

Radical hospitality provides an atmosphere in which the chain of stress and frustration may be broken, link by link. As one caught in this chain enters a home that extends Christian love, the sense of calm and order which that ministering family provides, even amid bustling activity, begins to filter out unnecessary stress and uncover the basic problems needing attention. For some, sitting down to a peaceful meal may be the beginning. For others, a complete night's sleep may begin to break the chain. Schedules and rules provide structure, eliminating further confusion and indecision about which way to turn and how to use one's time. Although the newcomer may at times chafe under this new structure, he will be redirected toward goals that bring genuine satisfaction and enable him to handle the pressures of everyday life.

Change does not come easily. But that is where the gospel of God's grace comes to vivid expression. The Christian family can introduce frustrated guests to that life-force Who alone creates the ability to change. God's gracious Spirit goes beyond our attempts to do things right, giving us instead the power to do so through salvation in Christ. To pressure one overwhelmed by stress to keep rules and regulations beyond his ability only adds more frustration and stress. It is here that the ministering family can offer both a haven in a heartless world and God's gift of grace to overcome failures and meet new goals.

In a very practical way, radical hospitality has as its goal an independent and yet God-dependent person living in, but not of, the world. For some who have suffered from a fear of rejection by others and have established patterns of great dependence, this means at first letting them know they are welcome and significant. Such an individual will usually be compliant, and yet fearful of failure. Here the ministering family must show appreciation for sincere efforts, while at the same time emphasizing the importance of doing all things ultimately for God's approval. If one belongs to God, significant steps toward success are possible, whether large or small. The host family can begin to withdraw its supporting influence as the person emerges with the right kind of inner strength and confidence.

For the super-independent person who enters the home of a Christian family, a different set of problems is created. This person is characteristically self-centered and considers others obliged to approve his actions and behavior. He basically feels that he knows what is right for his life, that he has been victimized by society or another individual, and that he will allow no one or nothing to stand in the way of reaching his goals. Very suspicious of all, he may lie to others and to himself so that his own ego may be kept intact.

For this independent-in-the-wrong-sense individual, radical hospitality often means a confrontation in a loving yet decisive way. Such a one, to make progress toward God's goals, must be shown his sin and his need of repentance, so that he may become a loving, considerate person.

Others may find it difficult to accept radical hospitality at first. Some have set patterns of withdrawal as they attempt to remain aloof, fearful that they may be hurt even more. Lacking a true sense of who they are, such people are easily threatened and react to these threats by even greater withdrawal. That withdrawal typically takes the form of retiring to one's room, sleeping a great deal, or appearing only at mealtimes.

The gospel of Jesus Christ is one of hope, and it is this hope which must be offered to the withdrawn individual. The ministering family can show unconditional love as they quietly encourage the newcomer to be a part of their family and join with them in everyday activities. We have found that playing a game together or working on a joint project very often accomplishes this feeling of acceptance.

To minister to the broken and hurting is a difficult task; to integrate them into a Christian home where they may see a model of Christ and the church is a continual challenge. People with new needs and hurts replace those who have found healing. There are always more people to care for. Mayor Koch's ten homeless are a token example of our society's woe.

Scripture has given a basis for the ministry of radical hospitality; society has accentuated the need; the Christian church is now called to action, so that bruised reeds may grow tall, and dim wicks may burn bright once more.

CHAPTER FIVE

"And There Are
Varieties of Ministries . . ."

Biblical commands to alleviate the practical and spiritual needs of hurting humankind need fleshing out. As we interviewed many during our preparation for this book, the variety of forms that radical hospitality may take became most evident.

Some who exercised this ministry lived in the inner city, some in the suburbs, some in the rural countryside. Some dealt mainly with teenagers, some with adults, still others with children, and a few with some of each. Some felt no limit to the number to whom they could effectively minister; others suggested a ratio of three adults to every incoming hurting person. For some, radical hospitality was their foremost ministry. For others, opening their homes was simply a small facet of the work God had called them to do. Yet, underlying each of these expressions of radical hospitality was an openness to the leading of God, to a change in focus, at times, and to a discipleship that was costly indeed.

We want to introduce you to four such ministering families, chosen not because they have opened their homes more often or more effectively than others, but because they simply represent the variety of focuses radical hospitality may have: in the city, in the country; ministering to many, ministering to few; providing short-term care, providing long-term care.

Bob and Jeanne Hall
The Bronx Household of Faith

"God has always had us living in big places," remarks Jeanne Hall, as she speaks of her family's involvement in radical hospitality. Bob and Jeanne with their three young sons are transplanted Minnesotans who have lived since 1973 in the southwest Bronx, just a block from one of the most heavily trafficked drug areas in New York City. Settled since 1976 in a large three-story, ten-room house, they are surrounded by apartment buildings and bordered by the decay that is synonymous with that region. Here God has led the Halls and two fellow Midwesterners, Jack and Pat Roberts, to establish and co-pastor the Bronx Household of Faith, a caring community of believers who reach out to a needy neighborhood.

Involvement with radical hospitality did not begin for the Halls when they moved to New York. During Bob's seminary days in St. Louis, they lived in a large apartment in a run-down section of that city. Modeling what they had seen in the lives of an older couple in the church they were attending, the Halls found themselves offering their extra bedroom to a friend's fiancée who needed a temporary home. She was followed by a young mother and her child, who, in turn, were replaced by a teenager.

As Jeanne and Bob reflect on those days, they remember

how their dining room became Bob's study, which worked well since they couldn't afford dining room furniture anyway. Those were the days of making their share of mistakes in trying to meet needs; they joke that one of their live-ins almost drove them to a separation and divorce!

When they arrived in New York City to minister in the Bronx, Bob and Jeanne found themselves with a two-bedroom apartment and a stream of newcomers rebounding from a breakup, deeply immersed in problems, or simply needing a place to be. When they looked for a home of their own, it was only natural for them to purchase the house that would make them backyard neighbors to Jack and Pat.

Originally, the focus of their new home was to provide a Christian community for those who sensed the call to be a witness in the urban sprawl and knew the necessity of living in proximity to one another. The two adjoining households became extended families, sharing their everyday lives and ministries.

Into their home came young adults needing love and direction. Others found their way from the neighborhood, wanting a new start. Those who asked to enter the household were advised of the required commitment to seek change in their lives, and still they came. The believers in each household provided a stable yet challenging home for the newcomers to grow. And for about four years this was the basic thrust of the Halls' radical hospitality.

In recent years, the focus of Bob and Jeanne's ministry has begun to change. One of those who had shared in the responsibilities of their house was led to a ministry in Brooklyn, necessitating a move on her part. The Halls found that God did not immediately send another worker to the South Bronx to replace her in their home. So foster care and adoption became another means of providing radical hospitality, and they brought into their home an infant and a teenager. The Halls have also shared their rooms as stopovers for returning missionaries and other Christian workers. Contacts over the summer led them to a large Kampuchean refugee population only a block and a half away. What was once an empty spare room has now become a distribution center for coats, shoes, and blankets donated by churches from the metropolitan New York area.

Without the support and care given them by their local church body, the Halls affirm, their home ministry would degenerate into being a crash pad. The Bronx Household of Faith has been for them a canopy under which they have been able to share shelter and Savior. When a teenager for whom they had struggled to provide love and acceptance angrily rejected their efforts and left, Bob and Jeanne were surrounded by a sympathetic, caring group. No one admonished them with an "I-could-have-told-you-so" attitude, but they came, as one woman did, with a sack of potatoes and onions, saying as best she could, "I know you are hurting; this is the way I can help." Without such expressions of care and prayer, the Halls acknowledge, the discouragement that accompanies rejection would have been devastating.

Living in the inner city and raising children in that environment has its high costs. Each morning the children from both households are transported west across the George Washington Bridge to Paterson, New Jersey, where they attend a cross-cultural Christian school. Nights bring the sounds of siren and ambulance. Yet Bob and Jeanne Hall refuse to think of themselves as special people. Instead, they practice what is their calling in the city—to be light in the midst of the darkness of sin and crime, hope in the hopeless cases of unemployment and despair, beauty in the midst of the ashes of broken relationships and lives.

As Jeanne Hall concludes, "We have the distinction of being the only ones in our neighborhood who can leave our door unlocked at any time. With so many people going in and out, burglars don't take the chance of coming face to face with a fellow human."

George and Louise O'Carroll
Outcault, New Jersey

About 35 miles southwest of New York City, in the flat, sandy, middle section of New Jersey, is the home of George and Louise O'Carroll. George, as if echoing Jeanne Hall, reflects, "We built a house bigger than we needed, not knowing why." For the last 15 years the O'Carrolls have learned why time and time again, as they have opened their home to those with countlessly diverse needs.

If one word could describe George and Wassy, as Louise prefers to be called, it would be *effervescent*. They are, above all else, people-persons who relate well to practically everyone they meet. For them, radical hospitality is just one of the many ways God has called them to share what they have and are.

George, a graduate of Gordon-Conwell Seminary, felt that his spiritual gifts would find their best use on a lay level. He took a secular job and began ministering through Bible studies focusing on teenagers and young adults, later expanding to include an effective outreach at a local retirement community. In addition, he was sought after for his counseling skills, and it was the experiences he had in counseling that led him to invite some of his counselees to live in his home, where they could witness a Christian family in action and find a more structured environment in which to work toward change. Wassy has her own ministries as well, establishing Young Life clubs in their area and operating a combination Christian bookstore and health-foods store in a nearby town.

The O'Carrolls do not actively recruit those who come to live with them; in fact, George tries to discourage some since he fears their motives may be faulty. Since he is concerned about his own family—a daughter in college and a son in high school—George first screens out any who may need more specialized counsel. These he refers to other agencies with whom he has an excellent working relationship. Secondly, the individual entering the O'Carroll home must have a job or be in school. With both George and Wassy employed outside the house, this is a must. George sees it as another indication that an individual is serious in his desire for help if he is willing to fulfill these conditions. Then, if the person has another option—if, for example, he can remain in his own home—the O'Carrolls encourage him to do so. They have no intention of creating a community of people who are dependent on them.

The O'Carrolls' home has provided shelter and restructuring for those in marital stress who need time apart so they can have a new start. George speaks of one young man to whom he and Wassy offered a second chance. George had been counseling the man, who was quite irresponsible, and his wife, who consequently wanted to end the marriage. By staying with the O'Carrolls, this young man was able to see a model worth imitating, something he had never seen in his own home as he was growing up. As the couple remained in counseling, and as George supervised the young man, the couple began to rebuild and were reunited after a four-month period of separation.

Another young girl had come East after leaving a difficult home situation in the Midwest. When she arrived in New Jersey, she found herself in an equally stress-ridden family.

She began to attend the O'Carrolls' Bible study, and Wassy soon asked her to live with them. In their home, this girl progressed rapidly, went to a Christian college, and met a young man to whom she will soon be married.

For each success there has been the pain of failure and being misunderstood. Resentment is a battle both George and Wassy have fought, whether it is the resentment, at times, of losing privacy or of being falsely accused. Yet, neither would send their household packing when these feelings arise. Opening his home to others has been a freeing experience for George—he finds himself to be less ruled by his feelings and much more objective as he deals with people. Susie, their college-age daughter, is now a sensitive, beautiful woman who echoes her parents' care for others. She herself has brought into their home those in need of loving concern. The respect that Wassy and George have from both those to whom they have directly ministered and those agencies with whom they have conferred is great and obvious. Yet, the ease with which they give themselves to others and the genuineness of that concern speak the loudest.

The house in Outcault is seldom quiet. The pace to which George and Wassy subject themselves is unrelenting. Their loving, yet direct, confrontation dispels the fog of dishonesty. In this home is life, and, as Jesus put it, the abundant life He came to bring.

Cliff and Barbara Adolphson
The Father's House, Lugoff, South Carolina

"Having Christ love others through us; that's what it's all about," writes Barbara Adolphson of the ministry she and her husband, Cliff, have in their home, which they have called The Father's House. Her words have been spoken from pulpit and mouthed by Christians time and again, but those words take on a special meaning in the Adolphsons' form of radical hospitality.

In the past four years, twenty children have found a new home and a new start as they have become part of The Father's House, some for extended stays, others for emergency overnights. Licensed by the South Carolina Department of Social Services as a therapeutic foster home, Barb and Cliff welcome into their family children and youths with emotional problems, helping to prepare these for adoption.

Until five or six years ago, the Adolphsons termed themselves a typical, successful, middle-class Christian family with three children in or approaching their teens. On a couples' retreat, their first weekend away from their children in 13 years, they began to examine seriously God's calling for their family. They found themselves drawn toward a more intensive ministry with youth than they had traditionally had and returned home determined to follow through with their renewed commitment.

Realizing that the first step for them was to have expanded space, Cliff and Barbara built a bigger home. In turn, they began to expand the love they would need as they ministered to some who had known only rejection.

Running a household with six or more youngsters requires organization. For the Adolphsons, this means the mundane task of posting chores so that all may learn responsibility. In addition, Barbara or Cliff works individually with each of their new family members, planning with him or her the changes necessary in each life. Here the gospel is presented both in word and through actions. Many have accepted Christ and have, in turn, been introduced to Christian families who have adopted them. Others have rejected Him and moved on.

The excitement of seeing a child awaken to love and acceptance cannot be captured in words. One of Adolphson's foster children was concerned about locating a half-brother who had been hospitalized in a state mental institution. As Barb and Cliff began to check through the bureaucracy, they located the then 11-year-old who had been assigned to that particular institution because no foster parents had been available to provide the care he needed. The Adolphsons welcomed him into their home, which he uses as a home base for vacations from the boarding school he now attends. His last visit home was a special one—he had his first ever birthday party at the age of 12 years, and the celebration ran high.

Another child, five years old, had disrupted eight foster homes before he arrived at The Father's House accompanied by his three-year-old sister, who thought she was his mother! The little boy was unable to speak more than single words because of a hearing deficiency. As Barbara and Cliff provided love and discipline, he was able to make astounding progress in speech therapy and in his overall behavior. God's love and healing again broke through almost impenetrable barriers.

Now with a total of four teenagers of their own, one of whom they were able to adopt after she spent time with them as a foster child, Barbara and Cliff Adolphson might be tempted to retire and wait out those years of teenage turmoil. While they do, at times, take a month or two break from their ministry to reestablish their own family, their devotion to God's calling remains constant. Neither knows when the ringing of the phone might signal the arrival of another of the lambs which God has called them to feed with His love and from His bounty.

Glen and Jean Hart
The Haft, New Albany, Pennsylvania

Glen Hart was working on his doctoral dissertation when shots rang out across the Kent State campus. Moments later, a student friend lay dying. It was then that Glen packed his books and returned to the Pennsylvania farm he and his wife Jean had struggled to restore when he retired from the Air Force 11 years before. That day in 1970 was a turning point in the Harts' lives, as they realized in a new way that God had called them to share what God had given them with any who were in need.

When the Harts had purchased The Haft in 1959, fifty years of sheep manure covered the ground floor of the barn. Only a man or woman with a vision could have seen beyond the shoveling and repairing that occupied the next several years. Subsistence living was the standard for those first years, a period Glen and Jean term their years of "learning and receiving" from the land, from helpful neighbors and friends, and from God.

In the years that have followed, Glen and Jean have occupied themselves with giving. The Haft is now a center for Christian community living with the accent on self-sufficiency, sharing, and conservation. It is a haven for those who want a new start in life, whether they be a confused teenager, a pregnant mother, a battered wife, a drifting alcoholic, or a young couple on the brink of a broken marriage.

Uniqueness of ministry best characterizes the activities at The Haft. In addition to the Harts, Michael and Joanne Carver, with their two young sons, and Beth Mack, with her preschooler, help in the tutor role. The others who come for help and a new beginning are termed students whether they be age 13 or 52. Glen Hart sees all of life as a learning process, and each student is encouraged to design his own educational plan, which includes education in its broadest sense.

Although the location of The Haft is described as remote, many find their way to its doors to begin anew. While the old sheep barn—now restored to a three-story structure providing housing, living space, kitchen, and storage areas— dominates the hillside, other buildings have been added in the years since the first hard struggles.

The Gatehouse, as it is called, is home for the Harts and any who might be transients, staying one or two nights. The Carvers live in the Shepherd's Cottage, where those who require the most care physically and emotionally are first housed.

Some of those who come to The Haft are recommended by pastors. Others find their way via state agencies and mental health offices. One woman came all the way from Venezuela through an amazing chain of events that began with a casual conversation in a Christian bookstore in New Jersey. The most dramatic arrival, according to Glen and Jean, was a young man who arrived at their doorstep high on drugs, with cuts on his neck and wrists. The only thing he remembered was being at a party in Philadelphia, hours away, when someone told him, "Man, you ought to go to The Haft." He had no recollection of how he had completed the trip or even where he was.

Those who stay at The Haft find unconditional love and guidance. It is not an easy life for many who are accustomed to the conveniences and accessibilities of suburban and urban life. Work is at times hard, but the changes are evident. As one young student wrote in a Haft newsletter:

I'm here at The Haft because I needed help getting my life straightened out. . . .

I came here August 26 and now it is December. I've
learned how to obey authority and communicate. But
most of all my life has become fulfilling, full of love and
contentment. . . .

. . . there's a difference between saying you've changed
and really changing. . . . If you're sincere, people will
notice the change. But you do have to be like a snake
shedding your skin to really live under God's love.

Glen himself comments on The Haft's remoteness, as
was reported in a July 17, 1981 article in *The Farmer's Friend:*

One of the major advantages of The Haft is its remoteness. We remove people from the temptations and we
feel this is necessary for most of our students. We deal
with all the social ills and all kinds of problems. We
don't shake-down or search people, but we believe that
by coming here, they are requesting help. If they slide
back into their old patterns, we confront them.

Many leave and later wish they had not. Others return,
seeking help again. For those who are tutors, life is de-
manding as they minister to many with deep problems. Yet
the depth of each tutor's relationship with the Lord is viv-
idly seen. For Joanne Carver, ministry has meant cutting
the blackened toenails of a Cuban refugee who had arrived
having no other place to turn. For Jean, it has meant innu-
merable trips to town for consultations with agencies and
transporting students for needed medical care. For all, it has
meant summers canning two thousand quarts of fruits and
vegetables, cutting untold cords of wood, and baking num-
berless loaves of bread. It has meant staying awake all night
with an alcoholic going through withdrawal. Radical hospitality at The Haft has meant assuming the mind that was in
Christ Jesus—that of a servant.

Christmas 1981 was a special one for the eight students

and seven tutors who gathered in the living room of the main barn. Dinner was turkey with the trimmings. Presents for each were carefully wrapped and placed under the tree. The fireplace crackled with a wood fire, sending warmth throughout the room. For some it was their first family Christmas ever.

The birth of Mary's child as celebrated at The Haft symbolized the new birth that has occurred countless times during these years of ministry. Mending broken lives has its costs, but as Glen and Jean put it, "God's gifts are so great that we must give away all we can and not think of anything else."

CHAPTER SIX

Self-Evaluation—
The Start

If the husband and wife aren't in this together, nothing can more quickly drive a wedge between them than this type of ministry.

I realized my own kid could end up in someone else's home getting himself together because of my involvement in this ministry.

Don't go into this ministry if you have anything you're afraid to have destroyed.

Christ taught His disciples the cost of discipleship, warning them that He was calling them not to a life of ease or acceptance. In the extended family ministry, the costs of radical hospitality are indeed high. A warm feeling of compassion is not enough to sustain you, nor is an objective conviction that a strong biblical foundation exists for such a ministry. Instead, you must realistically assess your own gifts and calling and, as important, your family relationship.

43

Overwhelmingly, those interviewed who had opened their homes to others in this radical way emphasized the grave risks of involving yourself in such a ministry without adequate evaluation and assessment. Too much is at stake for both your own family and the individual you welcome within your walls.

Dealing with Realities

Reality #1: *This Must Be a Joint Ministry of Husband and Wife.*

The first reality may seem to be obvious, but it cannot be stated strongly enough. Above all else, both you and your spouse must be in agreement that God wants you in this type of ministry. It cannot be one person's will superimposed on the other. This was repeatedly the emphasis of the couples interviewed.

Other factors in your relationship can, however, complicate the lives of those who agree to pursue this ministry. Consider together the following questions:

1. Do you compete with or complement each other? The competitor is always ready and available to correct the partner, so he or she can be known as the one who is right; the complementer is willing to fill the gaps. Those who have been most successful in extended family ministries tend to see partners playing the complementary roles of healer and confronter. One husband seemed to be able to provide the emotional support necessary for a broken individual, while his wife was able to cut through a situation and directly confront a habit such as laziness, which needed to be identified and changed. In another home, the wife gave emotional support, while the husband could emphasize that it

was important to do the right thing, hard though that choice might be. Neither partner did this in competition with the other; instead the complementary roles provided the needed balance.

2. How do you handle differences of opinion? This relates to the first question but differs slightly in that it affects your ability to solve problems as a couple. It's been said that if two people agree on everything, one of them is unnecessary. Yet it is important to work together to come up with a consistent approach to the new family member. Your partner may be able to be more objective about the newcomer. How do you react when you are confronted with another opinion?

3. Do you harbor grudges? The Ephesians 4:26, 27 passage—" 'In your anger, do not sin': Do not let the sun go down when you are still angry, and do not give the devil a foothold"—is a cardinal rule to be obeyed. Being at odds over personal issues or finances can only intensify the difficulties that come when another person is brought into the family scene.

4. What is your own relationship to Jesus Christ? This is another area that holds great import, since dependence on Christ is a total necessity in this ministry. One man related how daily he goes to his knees, asking God to order his day, and requesting, as is spoken of in James 1, wisdom in dealing with those in his home. We have found that one of us is usually God's means of encouraging the other to get through the added stress that comes with the entrance of the problem person.

Opening your home to another deepens your commitment to your partner. A young couple involved in a Christian community composed of extended families spoke of this deeper commitment they had experienced. Both were confident that God had led them to a rural Pennsylvania lifestyle. Both saw themselves as servants of each other as well as of God. Thus, when a new individual entered their home and problems arose, the husband and wife could not be pitted against each other in the struggle, but joined together to work toward a solution.

When an individual carrying great problems enters a Christian home, he is sure to see in real-life action what God intends for man and woman to be. Thus, if husband and wife are not working toward what they should be, a false picture arises. That's why the place to begin the evaluative process is with yourselves. Like the institution of marriage, the radical hospitality of the extended family is not "by any to be entered into unadvisedly or lightly, but reverently, discreetly, and in the fear of God."

Reality #2: *You Could Lose Your Own Child.*

Your own children and their reaction to bringing someone new into the family unit is a matter that should be carefully considered. In interviews both with host families and with their children this concern was foremost. Parents felt that next to their relationship with each other, the effect the ministry had on their children was by far the most significant area.

That God established the family as His unit for society is evident from Scripture, and the responsibilities of parents to their own children are spelled out in both the Old and New Testaments. Parents must first be certain they are dealing as well as they can with the known needs of the children God has entrusted to them before they reach out to minister to others.

At first, children, especially the younger ones, often welcome the addition to the family. In this way youngsters can be an asset to the ministry. Our kindergarten-age daughter treated everyone as an equal, showing no bias toward a handicapped person or a mixed-up teenager. If they were staying with us, they were, according to her, members of the family, and she just upped the number in our total household when she spoke with friends.

Still, there are considerations to be acknowledged. Difficulties do arise, even when you sincerely try to be sensitive to your children's needs.

1. One concern for some kids is that their mom and dad have more time for a newcomer than they do for their own children. A Bronx, New York family involved in a ministry to problem adults attempts to deal with this by scheduling family time apart from the rest of the household, spending time both in the home itself and by taking trips away from home. Another family uses Wednesday night as a family night, doing some activity on their own. Often the local church body will lend assistance by inviting the newcomer out, giving the host family a night off.

2. Other times, your own children may feel their privacy has been invaded. We found ourselves often using our daughter Kara's bedroom for those staying temporarily, since, with our son Kirk still sleeping in a crib, she seemed the most mobile. One day, however, we realized she wondered if she still had her own place, so the next newcomer was put elsewhere to ensure Kara's privacy. Older teens may not be so resentful or insecure. One college student whose parents had many staying with them understood the ministry to which her parents had been called and was at ease sharing her room and possessions. The key again is to be sensitive to your own children's feelings and needs.

3. A third problem encountered may surface when a younger child or teenager is taken into a family. One family,

in an attempt to make the new girl feel at home, encouraged the teenager to address them as Mom and Dad. Later they discovered their own children cringed at this, feeling that these titles of address were reserved for them. "Mom" and "Dad" had somehow been the signal that they were still special. This family decided that if they again took in a young person, they would find substitute titles for the parents.

4. A different type of concern involves the influence the new individual will have on your children. This should not be lightly dismissed, for it can be a genuine problem. Be observant and sensitive as to the amount of time the newcomer is spending with your children. Are the children becoming secretive? Is there a new vocabulary developing or new habits beginning to appear? If so, these must be dealt with in a loving, yet decisive way. Dealing with this negative influence may help your child to deal with the influence of the world outside the home. Discussing the situation with the child in an atmosphere that shows concern for the new family member may enable the child to feel a part of the family outreach.

5. Another area that causes resentment in children is the problem of lines of authority. It is essential that the new family member understand who is to discipline your child. Most parents prefer to take the responsibility on themselves, since the newcomer may be seen as a usurper and may not have similar standards, all of which can lead to inconsistency in the eyes of the child. We have made it clear to our children that they are first to listen to us, rather than follow another's directives.

6. Finally, the preadolescent and early adolescent years seem to be the hardest for children whose families are involved in this type of ministry. These are critical years of coming to terms with identity, and a sense of inferiority or

failure is a predominant feeling during this time for many children. In interviewing children of host families, those in this age group often voiced the feeling that they wished their parents didn't have others around, and that they felt their parents didn't have enough time for them. Some of this is normal adolescent perception, and the parents involved were aware of their children's feelings.

Two possible solutions may be proposed. Some families make a special effort to find time together during these years. When the complaint is then voiced by the teen, the parents remind him or her of the time they do spend together. The parents may often try extra hard to make the teen feel part of the family outreach. A second solution might be to take a sabbatical from the extended family ministry during these years of a teenager's life. Barb and Cliff Adolphson found that they need to take a month off every so often to reestablish their own four teens. As Barbara stated, "When we see Satan's pull on our own, we need to back up, to strengthen and uphold." This may be the only solution if a teen feels very deeply that he or she is being neglected.

A child often finds himself in a delicate balance between feeling loved and accepted and feeling unloved and rejected. Therefore, it is essential when you minister in an extended family that your own children constantly be reassured of your love for them through both action and word, so that in the end you don't gain the world and lose your own child.

Reality #3: *You Can't Hang on to Things.*

As we have opened our home in radical hospitality to others, we have had favorite china broken, photographs defaced, and tools left outside to rust. Our first reaction was anger, especially when the item had been a gift, was valuable in cutting down overhead, or had not come easily. David personally found himself cringing at long showers and lights left on, wastefulness we could not afford.

Again, there are considerations to ponder:

1. Your values are not the same as those of the person entering your home. Therefore, teaching and reorientation must occur. We learned the hard way that we often had to explain how to use items and where to return them. In this way, friction that may result from responsibilities not fully understood can be alleviated. While teaching responsibility is difficult, it is, without a doubt, necessary.

2. People are more important than things. Ruth, though a people-not-thing person, has had to reaffirm this truth when dishes or prized glasses are cracked and chipped by a well-meaning newcomer. She stops and reminds herself that to react with anger or dismay would only serve to devastate certain individuals.

3. People are to be accountable for their actions. This concept is perhaps the most difficult one to maintain consistently. This means confrontation, which most of us prefer to avoid, especially in the case of a deliberate action. It means establishing consequences for behavior rather than internalizing your frustration. It means taking time to handle feelings rather than letting them slip by.

When Ruth made a routine freezer check one Saturday morning, she was mystified to find only the top of a shoebox she had filled with homemade, goat's milk fudge the week before. Since our freezer often is in disarray and packages tumble out, she made a double search of the freezer itself and the surrounding area. David was involved in a work project with Danny, an older teen who had moved into our family two weeks before, when Ruth announced her loss. Danny laughingly assured her the fudge hadn't just walked away! Later, when Ruth climbed into the sleeping loft to locate a game for our daughter, she discovered the missing fudge next to Danny's bed.

Understandably, Ruth's immediate reaction was seething anger at Danny's stealing and subsequent lying. But she refused to lash out at him in her anger, refusing as well to let resentment begin to fester inside. Together we worked at confronting Danny, holding him accountable for what he had done. He offered no excuses and was scheduled to make a batch of fudge to replace the one he had stolen. By choosing to confront Danny, Ruth was freed from internal frustration, and he was held accountable for his behavior.

Basically, in this ministry, you have to remind yourself and your own children time and again of Christ's words that "a man's life does not consist in the abundance of his possessions" (Luke 12:15), but you are to "seek first the kingdom of God and His righteousness, and all these things shall be added to you" (Matt. 6:33 KJV).

Reality #4: *There's No Point Going into This for Glory.*

One of the realities of the extended family ministry is that, at times, it can open you up to all sorts of criticism. Charges of abandoning your own family, of creating your own cult, or harboring drug addicts and criminals may all be voiced. Your new family member will often resent your efforts to help him impose order in his life and may lash out. Your once quiet haven of a home may suddenly be filled with stress. Not every family entering this ministry gets named "Humanitarian of the Year." What should you consider?

1. Perfect children and perfect parents do not exist;

neither do perfect extended families. Adding a bruised and broken person to a family will only enhance the image of imperfection already present. The new family member may act up in public. The tendency may be to excuse the action and free yourself from embarrassment, since this is the problem kid. This is dangerous in the extended family, for the newcomer, hearing this, will mentally remain the branded child, the excluded adult. Rather than feeling more a part of the family, his sense of being on the outskirts is reinforced. In addition, the behavior, which should have been dealt with biblically, is glossed over rather than corrected.

2. Our identity must be found in the Lord rather than in what others think of us. The new family member may not be dressed the way we like, may not look attractive, may not even be an attractive person. Many of us, in turn, see this as a reflection on ourselves when we are seen with this new family member. Thus, we may feel awkward or fail to do what is right because of adult peer pressure, even pressure from within the church as to behaving in "proper ways."

David experienced this as he mentally compared the time we traveled and visited friends accompanied by an attractive, intelligent French exchange student and the contrasting Christmas we brought with us a man deformed in body and repulsive in personality. That holiday season we learned much of the glory, grace, and truth that Christ came to communicate as we became concerned more about this man's well-being and, after a struggle, less about how others might judge us because of him. We saw the rest of our family open up to him, not just tolerating his appearance in our Christmas celebration, but welcoming him into our traditional activities. Thus, we must allow God to teach us to overcome the world's status and prestige system, which places value on the outer rather than the inner man.

God's Calling and Leading

Step #1: *Seeing the Need*

Paul, in I Corinthians 12:4-6, reminds the church, "There are different kinds of gifts, but the same Spirit. There are different kinds of service, but the same Lord. There are different kinds of working, but the same God works all of them in all men." It seems as if there are an infinite number of ministries in which a believer may become involved. Each Christian, as an instrumental part of the body of Christ, has a particular ministry.

Those involved in an extended family ministry often cite "seeing the need" as one factor in God's using them in this way. As one put it, "This just seemed to evolve out of all the counseling I was doing. People needed a place where they could see a Christian model to imitate."

In our case, we also experienced the frustration of watching people we had counseled return to an unstructured environment, where they immediately suffered a relapse into past behavior. We sensed a need to have people stay with us, where we could talk with them on a day to day basis, encouraging them, rebuking them in love, all with the goal of reuniting them with their original families, if at all possible.

The call to this ministry, then, may grow out of acknowledging the need of the alien and the stranger (the Old Testament counterparts to the outsider and homeless) to be drawn into a family where they can begin or accelerate the process of being members of the family of God as they see radical hospitality in action. Thus, the Christian family is, to those outside, a model of the hope found in Jesus Christ.

Step #2: *Having Your Own Family Together*

Without a doubt your own family will bear the brunt of radical hospitality. Their ability to do so is obviously a consideration in determining the calling and leading of God.

Just as some who have psychological problems may go into the field of psychology in the hope of solving their own problems in the process, so others may enter into an extended family ministry in the hope of solving existing family problems. That is more than likely a false hope. The original family difficulties are not buried with the entrance of a problem person into the family. Instead, they intensify as a new element comes into the home. The new individual may sense some kind of division and begin to play one partner against the other. An incoming teenager may find it easy to manipulate one partner, leaving the spouse frustrated and upset. Children who feel their parents are neglecting them will only have those feelings intensified as the parents become involved in caring for the new family member.

A decision to become involved in an extended family ministry must be one that is discussed and agreed upon by all members of the family. Obviously, the input of a preschooler may be minimal, but he or she must be clearly informed of what the family plans to do. Without the agreement and understanding of the total family, disaster may loom ahead.

Step #3: *Adjusting to an Added Family Member*

In our case, we found the extended family ministry one into which we gradually grew. We became acquainted with this concept soon after we were married. At that time we realized that our involvement in such would be in the future, since we needed time to adjust to each other and begin our own family.

Our first step in opening our home to others on a long-term basis began three years later when we invited a stable, single young man in his mid-twenties, who was an active part of our church body, to live with us. Our original concern was to provide an inexpensive place for Blais, who was working with our church youth. Here he would be freed from working overtime to survive the high cost of living in our area. Ruth found little difficulty in cooking for one more, and this gave Blais additional time to prepare for his teaching ministry. During these next three years we learned to understand each other, talking through our problems in family meetings, adjusting our schedules, and dealing with the rough edges that needed to be sanded off each of us. We found great benefit in sharing expenses and the upkeep of the house, as well as balancing out childcare and weekly tasks. This grew into a positive sense of community, and another single young man came to stay as well. It was after this that God began to send us problem persons to whom we could minister, and we were, in many ways, now ready to open ourselves to this greater degree.

Others have found that opening their home to share meals or study together has been the preparation that led them into the next step of having someone live in their families. God again leads and prepares in various ways, but underlying all must be a willingness to open yourself to others in a radical, very difficult way.

Step #4: *Checking Improper Motives*

Sometimes we work hard at camouflaging our real motives for becoming involved in a project or ministry. While on the surface we may mumble something about wanting to help others or serving the Lord, we must be willing to consider some wrong motives that may actually be the reasons we want to become involved.

An insecure person may have an underlying motive to control or be in authority over others. A struggle begins when a troubled individual is introduced into such a person's home. The authoritarian may first try to coerce the new family member to behave according to a set of rules and regulations arbitrarily established to give the host an upper hand. At times he may bombard the newcomer with a long list of responsibilities without allowing him to have any say. In addition, such a host may rely on his own charisma, a forceful or winning personality, to create proper behavior. Unfortunately, or perhaps fortunately in the long run, the authoritarian often has a rude awakening when the newcomer reacts and refuses to submit. The authoritarian is then tempted to win at all costs, which, of course, is self-defeating, and all must suffer the loss.

Danny, introduced previously in the fudge incident, was one who ultimately chose to reject the structure we regarded as necessary to help him change. After we had repeatedly confronted him with his need to organize his time and had worked out ways for him to begin this, he continued his old ingrained pattern of irresponsibility, deliberately choosing to skip morning worship and hang out at the doughnut shop where he was employed. At that point we gathered his belongings and brought them to him there, since he had chosen not to submit to our authority. But, because we saw him as ultimately rejecting God's authority, we were freed from the frustration that accompanies the feeling that we had been used, and instead felt sorrow that Danny had not chosen God's way.

We must see that the power to accomplish change in a life belongs ultimately to God. While we have His power and authority entrusted to us, we must be careful to recognize the limits of our authority. Then we can handle the rejection of our authority and rest in knowing that the matter is in God's hands.

A second improper motive, touched upon in the "Realities" section, is self-glory. We think we will rise in the esteem of fellow Christians when they see us unselfishly opening our homes to others. The glory quickly fades when the problems and heartaches that accompany such a ministry are evident. The glory seeker is left in a dilemma: admit failure or prolong the difficulty by covering up.

When two fellows, both having deep problems, entered our home in the space of two days, members of our congregation expressed wonder at our ability to bring these into our family. The first day and a half we were caught up in the quick changes that had occurred, unsure of how God wanted to use us. By the evening of the third day, Ruth was ready to withdraw to any quiet corner, desperately needing a place for herself. The next morning was the Bible study she had been teaching, and she knew the women were anxious to hear of her progress. So she faced the question of whether to gloss over the difficulties that had arisen, thus maintaining an image that all was well, or to share the reality that we needed prayer support for direction and for coping. As she chose the harder way of admitting need, she found new freedom to love and welcome our new family members, despite the added frustration.

These improper motives, if discovered and checked as you enter this ministry, will not be able to wreak the damage they otherwise could. One more stress area can be removed.

Step #5: *Evaluating Your Physical Circumstances—Time, Space, Health*

Time: As has been stated before, time is a fixed commodity. Each of us has 24 hours a day. Lack of time is a malady that plagues us all. In radical hospitality, time, or the lack of it, is one of the greatest concerns, which is one of the reasons this book advocates, as an ideal, a family ministering to just one person at a given time.

In essence, working with a problem person of any age within the atmosphere of the home is indeed raising a child to maturity. Time must be spent teaching, working out a schedule, supervising, and evaluating. Naturally, the amount of time needed with an individual will vary, depending on his or her age and stability, but time must still be considered one of the determining factors in assessing your involvement in this ministry.

Supervision is another important matter, and here some practical matters must be considered. If the wife is the one who will spend the most time with the newcomer, it is probably best to limit your family to working with a child or a female adult. As a pastor, David has been able to work out of our home and thus have the time to supervise a male between studying, visiting, and counseling. Another pastor involved in radical hospitality had his new family member work at the church and then return with him at the end of the day. Still another solution to this dilemma is to have the problem adult employed in an outside job during the day.

Often a person with deep problems finds it difficult to

make choices. Then time must be taken to teach the necessity of responsible action. This means spending time helping him or her structure evenings, chores, and free time, all with the goal of giving him independence.

In beginning an extended family ministry, it might be wise to limit other church responsibilities until the home ministry can be established. The local church body must recognize the calling in this area and see this aspect of the ministry of the saints. Whether other ministries are eliminated or not, the extended family outreach deserves primary attention.

Space: Obviously, a three-room apartment with three occupants at present will probably not provide the space necessary for having an extended family ministry. Many of us, however, fail to be creative with the space we do have.

For a family who may have a large home with unused space in the attic, basement, or wherever, or those who may, like us, own a large barn with plenty of room for expansion, the extended family may be the best way to use that potential to its fullest rather than cluttering the extra space with junk. There are many ways we can rearrange our homes if we are willing to be concerned about people, rather than maintaining society's concept of a middle-class home.

During one winter when oil costs soared, we decided to move our family from the downstairs bedrooms, which were heated by oil, to the upstairs living area, which was heated by a wood stove. We would bed the children in the loft built in the peak of the barn, and we would sleep in the hide-a-bed on the main floor. Our plans for not using our oil burner changed rapidly as God brought an additional person into our family to use one of the vacated bedrooms. We found God teaching us to trust Him for the finances for the oil and not allowing us to fall into the trap of being unwilling to use what He had provided us in a home. In reality, the move upstairs was a means for us to maintain a degree of privacy. By being flexible, we were able to make the additional space available for this young man's need.

Health: Those interviewed for the book all mentioned the fatigue that often accompanies ministering to broken individuals in such an intensive way. Having a major illness in the family limits the amount of available energy and time that can be given to a problem individual. This factor must also be carefully considered.

Conclusion

We are surrounded by needy people. As Christians we have a responsibility to minister to these needy ones. Yet, we have a God who calls and leads us into the areas where we can best serve. In considering involvement in a ministry in an extended family, we must realistically come to terms with the price that such a service exacts, but we must also be sensitive to the still, small voice that confirms the way we should go.

Activities

1. As a husband-wife team, first respond separately to the questions below, then discuss your answers together.

> How do I evaluate my own commitment to Jesus Christ?
> In a relationship, am I usually the confronter or the healer?

What strengths does my partner possess in the above areas?
How do I respond when my ideas are challenged?
What needs do our own children have at this time?
What time, space, and health limits do we have?
How can some of these limits be dealt with creatively?

2. Together explore why you might feel led into radical hospitality. Read Isaiah 58:6-12 and Luke 14:12-14, listing biblical principles for this ministry.

3. List any fears or qualms you now have as you look into this ministry. What are the attributes of God from which you could gain strength? What scriptural promises could calm your fears?

CHAPTER SEVEN

Is This the One? Or Should We Look for Another?

You've dealt with the realities of the extended family ministry. You've sensed God's leading and direction toward this radical hospitality. Now, where do you find that person who will become a part of your family?

Circumstances under God's Control

If the extended family is under the authority of the local church, then that Jerusalem, the local body, is logically the place to begin. Saints ministering to saints can grapple together and meet needs, working toward the ideal in Acts 4:34, having no needy persons among them.

Perhaps one of the most successful experiences we have had in the extended family ministry came about in this way. One of our church teenagers had become quite despondent, troubled at home and ready to drop out of school. She and her divorced mother, both a part of our church body, needed time away from each other. Kathy came to stay with us weekdays, returning home for weekends. During this time we kept in daily contact with her mother and had the additional benefit of prayer support from the entire church.

Another church family, overwhelmed with the health problems of two of their children, needed time apart from an adopted daughter who was reacting unfavorably because she did not feel fully accepted. For nine months, Barbie lived with a young couple who had extensive experience working with emotionally disturbed children, and during that time was able to reach the point of being successfully reunited with her own family.

Other extended families have had similar experiences. At times an older teenager or young adult might attend a home Bible study. From this, as needs become evident, the move from a weekly counseling session to a daily living situation may be smoothly accomplished. This has often been the case in the family of George and Louise O'Carroll. Whatever the circumstances, you don't often have to look far for someone who needs the shelter of a Christian home.

Referrals also come from other Christians. A telephone call might announce, "I've got someone here I think you might help." A friend from outside your area might know a person who not only needs a Christian home, but also a totally new environment. We have used Christian families in rural Pennsylvania when it seemed part of the teenager's problem centered in the school he was currently attending.

Some Christian extended families have also had referrals from state agencies. At Berachah Farm, in the hills of Pennsylvania, Malcolm and Jessie Eldredge were requested by the state to take two foster children who had spent much time in state institutions. The transformation of the two children, especially the little girl, from frightened, animal-like youngsters to happy, playful kids was indeed a work of

God's grace, sought with much prayer and toil on the part of the Eldredges.

Then there are those who just show up on the doorstep, referring themselves, as it were. They may have heard about you from someone along the way. They may be just looking for a handout, but they arrive. Few families in this ministry are without takers for their openness and hospitality.

The Necessary Sense of Peace

While finding people who want to join your family is not difficult, welcoming the one to whom God would have you minister on a radical basis is another story. Here the peace of God must rule in your heart.

The extended families we interviewed found themselves divided on this issue of accepting anyone who came to them. Some, like John and Ruth Vandegriff of Howell, New Jersey, felt they would accept anyone who showed up, but in the course of the ensuing two or three days would begin to screen the newcomer. Since their extended family is under the authority of the local Bible Fellowship Church, and others in the church are also involved in this type of ministry, they could then refer the newcomer to another place if their own home did not seem to be the right one. At the rural Pennsylvania Christian community, The Haft, it is their basic policy to accept all who come, believing that God will do the screening process and send on those who cannot be helped.

On the other side of the issue are those who prefer to screen potential family members before accepting them. At Berachah Farm and in the family of Bob and Jeanne Hall, the ministering adults sit down with the prospective newcomer and seek a unanimous confirmation from the Lord that this person can best be served by the family. In both cases, the newcomer is given an initial interview, during which time he or she must agree to live under the terms the family has set.

If the extended family is under the jurisdiction of the local church, confirmation by the elders is another helpful and, in a sense, necessary step. Meet with them to explain what you hope to accomplish and seek their approval. Above all, as you weigh all the relevant factors, you must seek the Spirit's confirmation that He is in the decision and will do a great work. Everyone who comes will be a learning experience for you; your step of faith carries with it risks for all involved. That is why God's peace, which can come only when those ministering are in agreement, must be sought.

Background Research

"We just didn't think of going back and checking with the children's home. We just got on with the business of ministering," commented one mother involved in an extended family ministry.

Under the heading, "What I Wish I Had Known Before I Started," this checking on background came up frequently. Out of ignorance, and overwhelmed by the great visible need, many extended families fail to gain background information that would have been invaluable down the line.

When a broken individual enters your home, your first glimpse of his shattered world is through his eyes. It is possible to invest a great amount of time, energy, and emotion in trying to help this person before realizing that there is more to his story. Making a thorough background check is an essential first step to avoid misdirecting your efforts.

Contact the family of the newcomer—parents, brothers and sisters; check with his school if he is of that age; call any social agencies that might have had contact with him; speak with other Christians who may know him. This information is not a collection of gossip or ammunition, but will give you a more rounded outlook on the person, helping you pinpoint manipulation, alerting you to possible dangers, letting you know past behavior problems. Even negative input can be helpful in signaling why the child or adult wished to escape his natural family.

During one winter we had two young men come to stay with us in the period of two days. By the time we were able to run a background check on both of them, the teenager had stolen medication from the older of the two. As we checked with the state agencies, we discovered that Randy, the teenager, had a long police record and was on probation for theft. He had been placed in an out-of-state foster home, which he had left. With our new knowledge, we could deal more effectively with him, watching our possessions and putting more controls on him. Although he chose to leave our home rather than live within structure, we were able to deal with his behavior and confront him on this. The older man, an epileptic, had developed patterns of manipulation, which we later had confirmed as we spoke with his family. Had we contacted his family sooner, we might have been able to deal with this problem from the start.

As mentioned before, our dealing with Kathy, our church teenager, was extremely successful, since we were able to maintain contact with her mother, as well as check with her school guidance counselor and the social worker/counselor who services our church. With all of us working together, Kathy was able to return home within five or six weeks having a much healthier relationship with her mother.

While, at first, you may be squeamish about making all

the telephone calls, or perhaps feel like a private investi-
gator, God calls us to work with truth, and truth means
getting the facts. That way, you can achieve the most coop-
eration as you work toward making the new family member
independent or reuniting him with his nuclear family.

Establishing Living Terms and Goals

An extended family ministry is not a boarding house.
Those who are part of the family must agree to the terms of
the family. Again, this was a strong point in our interviews.
When someone enters your family, there are certain basic
terms that he or she must understand and to which he must
give assent for radical hospitality to be successful. The three
areas most generally agreed upon are as follows:

1. A purpose for coming.
2. The recognition of and submission to authority.
3. A willingness to work toward change.

1. Why is the troubled person here in your home? While
that question may sound trite, it is perhaps the most important consideration. It will enable you to establish both
the purpose and the duration of his stay.

What are his goals? What needs does he have? By answering these questions, both you and your new family
member will be able to evaluate progress or regress, keep-
ing in mind the ultimate goal of his achieving independence
or being reunited with his natural family. A weekly private
session to evaluate progress and discuss problem areas is
most productive, but without a sense of purpose and direction you will deal in generalities, wasting time and creating
a stagnant situation.

The rest of your family will also be able to minister to each

other and the newcomer to the extent that they, too, understand the goals toward which your new family member is
working. As he makes progress in various areas, the others
in your family can give praise and affirmation. They can
pray for him in his struggles. And as you help him establish
his place in the family, he will begin to feel a part of your
home and not an outsider.

Setting goals may not be an easy exercise for either you or
your new family member, but without it ministry becomes
almost meaningless, and a boarding house mentality may
result. Obviously, in the case of a child or teenager who is
seeking help, the natural parents should also be involved in
setting goals, but input from the child cannot be ignored.

Doing such an exercise will help you avoid a situation
in which we found ourselves. With one young man, we
failed from the beginning to establish a purpose for his stay
with us. While we wanted to deal with the whole person,
spiritually, emotionally, and physically, our guest wanted
only physical shelter and human companionship. When we
later began to confront him on changes needed in his life, he
objected; he had not known what was expected of him.

By establishing someone's purpose for coming, you may
also be able to set a time goal for leaving. While not an
inflexible deadline, it will help to give direction and an
objective. Otherwise, families have found the person never
wants to achieve independence, preferring to stay in the
comfortable confines of the home.

2. Will the newcomer submit to your authority? This is
the second key question that must be asked. Without agreement on this matter, only frustration will result. Your own
children will find it hard to understand why they must obey
while the new family member can do as he or she pleases.
Loving authority, as opposed to authoritarianism, estab-
lishes and enforces the basic family policies.

One family, finding that their authority was constantly challenged by a particular girl staying with them, had to ask her to leave, since that was the best solution for all. Because God demands obedience to legitimate authority, that ingredient must not be neglected in a ministering home. At the same time, the host family must patiently realize that a newcomer may need gradually to learn how to obey, if obedience has not been a part of his or her past.

Dave Pollock, director of Interaction, Inc., in Brattleboro, Vermont, who with his wife Betty Lou has shown this radical hospitality many times, emphasizes the need for Matthew 18:15-17 to be the rule as you exercise God's authority. When difficulty does arise, you must first deal with each other and then, if necessary, bring in an arbitrator. If the issue is not resolved, the church is to be involved. This way, if your newcomer accuses you of authoritarianism as you exercise God's authority, you have a check system that can still potential criticism.

3. Is your new family member willing to work toward change? Once goals have been established, and submission to authority is understood, the remaining question involves willingness to work toward change. The phraseology, *work toward change,* rather than just *to change,* is important. While God's grace alone gives the power to effect real change, an individual must be consciously willing to obey God's law. Habits are not easily broken, and change often comes slowly. The emphasis, then, must be on making a responsible effort toward that end.

As you see positive change, you must commend this, praising your newcomer's progress and reinforcing his steps toward growth. This is especially important as the newcomer stays past the first few weeks, and familiarity, as the adage goes, breeds contempt. Do not take progress for granted, but continue to encourage greater gains.

Affirmative answers to the three questions above will not ensure a problem-free stay for a newcomer in your family. But an agreement on these points will enable you to handle the struggles that arise. When the rough edges resist God's sanding, you may have to go back to these initial questions and reaffirm that the goals are well worth the discomfort. Then your vision of a stable, productive man or woman who finds contentment and happiness in God will once again appear within the realm of possibility.

Sending Him on

Admit limitations. That is another cardinal rule of showing hospitality in a radical way. We are not all gifted counselors. Some problems are beyond our understanding. God in His sovereignty often chooses to use many people in bringing an individual to Himself.

Most extended families avail themselves of other resources. A medical doctor can determine if a problem is physical. Christian counselors and social workers can provide in-depth treatment. Other extended family situations, which may use a different approach from yours, may be able to deal more effectively with the person you find hard to reach.

Compile a list of rescue missions, halfway houses, rooming houses, and other living facilities that may be helpful as the person moves on. Talk with social service agencies for other possible treatment centers.

If the new family member will not submit to your authority or refuses to change, the only solution often is to ask him to leave. Sometimes the greater lesson is learned when he realizes that actions do have their consequences.

The Vandegriffs told of a woman who was staying with

them and refused to get to her job on time. Despite their attempts to help her change, she continued to be late, eventually losing her job. They then realized she would have to leave their home. Forcibly removing her from their home, John and Ruth took her to the Salvation Army, where they paid for one week's stay. Ruthie's initial reaction to their seeming failure was tears, but both of them came back to John's overriding basic tenet of the extended family ministry—doing the right thing is the most important.

Conclusion

God is in the business of re-creation. As you participate in that work in the extended family, the person He sends you must see a need and want to change. This is not an automatic response. It must be nurtured through love and acceptance as you open your home in this radical way. However, unless you keep in mind the ultimate goal and are willing to bear with the struggles and setbacks, you may end up with the easy wood, hay, and stubble, rather than the difficult gold, silver, and costly stones.

Activities

1. Look at your own local church body. What needs do you see that might be best met by exercising radical hospitality?

2. React to the statement, "The extended family ministry is not a boarding house." What are the differences between exercising radical hospitality and running a boarding house?

3. Steve Smith, an 18-year-old who has been thrown out of his own home for failure to live within his parents' rules, asks if he can stay with your family until he can find a room elsewhere. What steps would you follow in making your decision?

4. Make a list of available resources in your area that would be helpful to an extended family.

CHAPTER EIGHT

Parents—
The Other Side of the Coin

Whenever someone enters an extended family, he does not come alone. Accompanying him is the baggage of his own natural family. The incoming adult usually has left-over, unresolved failures in relationships; children bring their present difficulties. The individual cannot be treated in a vacuum. That is why you, as the extended family parents, need the input from the other family members and especially from parents.

As you work with an adult, his parents can be helpful in sharing the past—what they have done, how he has re-acted, what successes he has known, what failures. From this information you may be able to go on to help your new adult family member begin to find healing and ultimate freedom from the baggage of these unresolved failures that have saddled him for so long.

Just as independence is the goal for the adult in the extended family, reuniting the child with his natural parents is the intent for the minor.

Seeing the Parent's Perspective

More than once David has sat listening to a teenager's tale of woe that led him to become enraged at the parental cruelty the teen was enduring. However, as he then contacted the parent and began to discuss the situation with him, David often saw that what was interpreted by the teenager as parental cruelty was more often a faulty attempt on the parent's part to correct the teen's improper behavior.

Discernment is a most necessary gift as you engage in the extended family ministry. "Praying for wisdom" is not a pious phrase. It is important to see both the parents' and the child's perspectives on the family problems that have led to division.

Each of us has an uncanny native knack of seeing life from his own perspective. Adam and Eve did this in the garden when each refused to take responsibility for his or her own sin—he blamed her, she blamed the serpent. A child may think his parents are at fault and demand that they change, while the parents see just the reverse. You need to listen carefully to both to enable each to see how his adversary understands the situation.

One man who stayed with us had been thrown out of his mother's house for no reason, or so he claimed. Then the police stopped by our door armed with a restraining order, forbidding him to contact his mother. When David tried to reach the mother, she would not come to the phone. After the man had been with us a short time, however, and David was able to contact his brother, we began to understand that his mother had not been cruel. This man had developed the attitude that said, "You do for me, you owe it to me." As he stayed with us, any attempts on our part to have him take responsibility were thwarted as he tried to make us feel guilty for making any demands. When he left us, he returned to his mother's home, where they resumed battle.

Because parents may feel guilty and not handle their failure correctly, it is essential to listen carefully to what they say. Even though they may take severe actions toward their children, your awareness of such actions and the motives behind them can afford helpful insight into a child's real problems.

Building Relationships

Failure is difficult to face. Parents who place their children in another's home are keenly aware that all has not gone well in their own home. Some experience relief that a stormy situation may subside. Others turn antagonistic and seem to be bent on causing the child to fail in the new home situation. Others are embarrassed and apologetic. And some even reach the point where they honestly don't care. In any case, you, as the extended family parent, must be extremely sensitive about building a relationship with parents whenever possible.

In your favor, you probably have credibility in the eyes of the parent. He or she, otherwise, would not have agreed to this placement. You have stated that your goal is to reunite parent and child. You are not out to start an off-beat cult with someone's child as hostage. All of these reminders can help.

The parents who had placed their children in extended families had as a major complaint, as we interviewed them, a lack of communication regarding what was happening with their children. Granted, their perspectives may have been clouded by mixed emotions, but this lack of communication is an issue which must be considered. As you set bounds with the parents, you must always remain sensitive to the fact that God holds *them* ultimately responsible for their children, and therefore you want to help them live up to that responsibility.

Establishing Bounds

As parents temporarily transfer to the ministering family their responsibility for their children, there must be an accompanying transfer of authority. Berachah Farm has set up a written agreement, which is here reproduced to give guidelines spelling out the terms of authority.

Form #1, 7-9-79 3A

TEMPORARY TRANSFER OF CUSTODY
FAMILY RESOLVE

We resolve as a household to function as a body and a family. The expression of love, either confrontive or supportive being the foundation. We desire Christ as our love source, thus allowing failure without rejection. We choose unity, and agree to resolve difficulties rather than ignore them.

We see family activities and allowing time to know each other, communicating ideas and enjoying each other, as vital to our lifestyle. We purpose to provide no obstacles, but to speed each other on to the intimate knowledge of God.

Scott Eldredge, November, 1977

A. *Agreement:*

This agreement is made this _____ day of _____

month

_____ A.D. between _____

year   husband & wife or guardian

_____

son, daughter, complete name

and Berachah Farm, wherein for a minimum period of six months, the complete responsibility for housing and training, etc. of _____ will become the sole responsibility of Berachah Farm staff, under the supervision of the Board of Directors.

B. *Specific Stipulation of Agreement:*

1. Parents are encouraged to visit the child, by making prior arrangements with the director.

2. The director and staff will cooperatively decide when a child will be permitted to visit their parents, and the length of time of visit. This will depend upon the child's progress and adjustment.

3. In the event of serious illness or accident, parents will be contacted immediately. In the meantime, Berachah Farm will have the authority to take any necessary action. When the child requires the professional help of a doctor, etc., parents will be responsible for all medical expenses.

4. Clothing, spending money, toilet articles, etc. are to be supplied by the parents. No cigarettes, tobacco, drugs, etc. are permitted at Berachah Farm (1 Corinthians 3:16-17).

5. It is fully understood by the child *"that they want to be here"* to receive help and direction for their lives. If there is consistent disobedience or unwillingness to cooperate on the part of the child, the director and staff with the approval of the Board of Directors may

recommend that the child be returned to the parents or guardian.

6. It is understood by the parents or guardians and the child what the ministry and purpose of Berachah Farm is composed of:
   1. *Living together as a family* (Philippians 4:8, 9)
   2. *Working together in unity* (1 Thessalonians 5:12, 13)
   3. *Studying and growing in the wisdom and knowledge of God and His Word* (2 Timothy 3:16, 17).

   It is further understood that the child *is required* to participate and function in *all the areas* of the ministry.

7. The primary goal of Berachah Farm (under God) is to guide and direct the child into a vital and intimate relationship with Jesus Christ, through His Word, the Bible, so that the child will find purpose, direction and meaning in life. As the Holy Spirit accomplishes His purposes in the child, it is the desire of Berachah Farm and the staff to return the custody of the child to the parent or guardian.

8. If the child is of school age and is educable, Berachah Farm will make arrangements with the local school district (Sullivan County) to provide for continuing education. All expenses and fees are to be paid by parents or guardians.

9. It has been estimated by the Berachah Farm Board of Directors, that it costs approximately $35 to $40 per week, to feed and house an individual child. Realizing this, and knowing my financial situation, I am willing to commit myself to giving _____ on a monthly basis.

   _{amount}

We as parents and our child have read the above "Temporary Transfer of Custody" to Berachah Farm and fully realize the responsibility and implications involved, and will endeavor to cooperate with the director, the staff, and the Board of Directors, to facilitate, under God, a timely return of our child as a well adjusted member of our family and society.

Under the "good yoke"

Accepted   Rejected   _____

Date _____ Date _____   Parents', Guardian's Signature

_____
Child's Signature

Reasons:

_____
Director's Signature

A written agreement such as the preceding one is a means of having an objective document, which can be used as a reference as questions arise. Coming to terms at the beginning of a child's stay is vital in avoiding misunderstanding.

Many extended families discourage parent contact or involvement for a period of time. They believe a child needs a clean break from the old patterns, and if the child and parents are reunited too soon, the old system is reinforced.

Others, in the setting of the local church, begin to have the child return to his home first on weekends, then adding weekdays, carefully evaluating what progress has been made. In the case of Kathy, our church teenager, we encouraged her mother to telephone, since Kathy needed reinforcement from her. Another time, we discouraged a teenager who was staying with us from calling home, once we discovered he was using the telephone as a weapon against his mother. In his case, we allowed him to call only when one of us was present, and he had written out what he wanted to say.

The definitive issue to be resolved with parents, then, is your authority over their child while he is in your custody. To subject the child to be torn between two conflicting authorities is cruel.

Counseling for Parents

Since all family members contribute to a problem within a family, it is wise for the natural parents to become involved in counseling as well. You as the parent in the extended family may find the natural parents seeking you out for counsel. While their seeking is a good step, which should be encouraged, it is better for them to seek outside counsel since your time will be limited with your other responsibilities. An outside counselor also has a degree of objectivity you lack.

This counselor can also be invaluable as you contribute your input as to the child's progress in your extended family. Eventually the goal is to bring all the family members into counseling so that parents and children can be taught healthier, biblical responses.

In our situation, we utilize a Christian social worker, who meets with both parent and child. Barbie, the ten-year-old adopted girl, began to see our social worker before the placement was made in the extended family. The social worker and pastor suggested this placement and then continued to give support to Barbie, her natural parents, and her extended family parents. Change came slowly, but now, two years later, the family is handling its difficulties in better fashion, and Barbie, who has been reunited with them, is doing well.

Problems Parents Create

Although parents may be relieved that their difficult child is now elsewhere, this does not alleviate their guilt. That can be cared for only as they see the forgiveness God offers to those who repent and believe. Guilt that is ignored surfaces in different reactions. The extended family parents must be aware of at least two of the possible forms such reactions may take.

Jealousy

If you succeed where they as parents have failed, jealousy will be an initial reaction. One teenager came to us after running from his home and refusing to return. With us, he began to succeed where he had known failure before. At first, his mother was glad to have him stay since she was unable to control him. As part of his room and board, we had him cut our grass. We found an old bike for him to fix up. Everyone had always called him stupid but had never taken the time to patiently teach him skills.

Dave and he would work on the bike; he would do some chores, and then, as a reward, they would go somewhere together. Soon this boy, who previously had entertained himself by throwing rocks through windshields and picture windows, was extremely helpful and pleasant. A real breakthrough came when he asked for help in doing a chore—he previously always said he knew how to do things in order to compensate for his feelings of stupidity.

The problem came when his mother stopped by. When she inquired how her son was doing, she was amazed that we did not have a negative report. Then the truth of the matter hit home with her—she was a major cause of her son's problem. She became defensive and jealous, returning the next day and making him leave.

This was one of our first ventures into this ministry, and with more insight we might have handled the matter differently, becoming more sensitive to her problem. Then she might have allowed her son to continue to progress, rather than seeing him later arrested for stealing and wrecking a van.

Another mother was incensed that her daughter asked the mother in the extended family for permission to go somewhere before she checked with the natural mother. While this really was the natural mother's insecurity and improper reaction, it is important for parents in the extended family to emphasize and reemphasize to the natural parents that they are not trying to replace them as mom and dad, but are temporarily helping out.

You, as the extended family parent, may be able to lessen the potential for jealousy by quietly reminding the natural parents that, in a sense, the stakes of failure are not as high for you as they might be for them. Bob Hall reminds us that the natural parents are "inextricably bound to their child and his problems for the rest of their lives. The extended family parents can send the child away, admitting failure, but usually in the sense that their particular situation could not meet the need of that particular child. The natural parent has no such option. The extended family parents can 'walk away' from the situation. The natural parents cannot." Showing yourself as a fellow struggler may change a jealous parent from enemy to ally.

Anger

Anger is another response that grows out of parental failure. Usually it takes the form of criticism, a commodity generously heaped on extended families. Again, when you begin to make progress with a child, you may find that natural parents instead find fault with your most insignificant blunders in an attempt to discredit you in their minds.

This is another time when the extended family parents often have to take the initiative in thwarting the anger by being open with the parents and encouraging them to rebuild the bridges with their child. When this does not work, you must find comfort from the knowledge that you have tried, "if it is possible, as far as it depends on you [to] live at peace with everyone" (Rom. 12:18).

You will, at times, make mistakes, and the natural parents may be quick to celebrate your fall. Yet, as you lovingly deal with the parents and attempt to let them know how you are operating, they may soften and begin to work with, rather than against, you and their child.

Conclusion

Children who leave their natural families for a new start in an extended family often have known stress, tension, and open hostility, feelings shared as well by their parents. Since the quest of the host family is not to transplant problems, radical hospitality calls for those engaged in it to be listeners, to see past the immediate reaction to the long-range healing. As you focus on the goal of reuniting the family, minus the problems with which the child left, parents will usually see it is for their best interests to co-operate and work together rather than to thwart your efforts. Then their propensity to control and manipulate can be defused.

Activities

1. What factors might thwart good communication between the extended family and the natural parents? Who, do you think, should initiate such communication, and why?

2. What biblical principles do you see in the Berachah Farm Family Resolve form (pp. 76-79)? What are the responsibilities of the parents? The child? The staff at Berachah? Why would such a form be helpful when parental guilt arises?

CHAPTER NINE

Mucking It Out

The sun rises every morning and sets every evening. Autumn is followed by winter, spring, and summer. Jesus Christ is the same, yesterday, today, and forever (Heb. 13:8). Man is destined to die once, and after that comes judgment (Heb. 9:27).

These are certainties in life. Just as certain as these, exercising radical hospitality through the ministry of the extended family will mean much time spent "mucking it out," or getting through each day with its confrontations, skirmishes, agreements, and victories.[1]

This chapter is gleaned from the experiences of many in this ministry who have opened their homes to the bruised, battered, and broken. Yet, as one of those interviewed

---

1. The phrase "mucking it out" goes back to the construction trade, where it refers to removing unstable mud and silt and exposing a solid bed of rock or granular material upon which to start roadbed construction. Until the bed is mucked out, the area shifts and sinks and cannot support heavy-bed materials.

remarked, "We can share experiences, but as Christians we first need to see what the Scripture says." Your everyday dealings with an individual in an extended family must be based on God's Word.

Beware! Manipulation Ahead

Most of us who deep inside have some kind of drive to be people-helpers unfortunately entertain at the same time a romanticism that assumes that if we only show we care and make life easier for a struggling fellow human, he will miraculously respond and all will be content forever. As Christians, we must first remind ourselves of the reality of the fall. As a friend succinctly put it in remarking about his year-old son, "Beauty is skin-deep, but depravity goes straight to the bone." Man's heart is more "deceitful than all else and is desperately sick. Who can understand it?" (Jer. 17:9, NASB). Ministering in the extended family requires a belief in the sinfulness of man. Then the ministering family will not be shocked when the new family member does not always respond positively to them, or they to him.

One interviewed family put it this way: "Expect manipulation; people will take advantage of you." Just as children in a family soon learn which parent is an easy mark, so the newcomer to your family will soon sense your weakest link. If one partner is extremely empathetic, he or she may soon be the target of an outpouring of heart-rending woe. If the other partner is the "hard guy," enforcing rules and regulations, he or she may be attacked as the unreasonable dictator, all in hopes of arousing guilt feelings.

Children coming into an extended family many times bring with them habits of lying and deception. These techniques have been effective in the past and are not easily changed. They must, however, be confronted and changed.

It is advisable, when a child enters an extended family, to have him undergo a complete physical checkup, if economically feasible. In this way, you will be aware of any medical conditions present and of any past abuse the child may have experienced. This can be to your advantage later if the child, after a confrontation on his unacceptable behavior, accuses you of abuse in hopes of being taken out of your home.

Manipulation must be handled with firmness and love. To allow it to continue unchecked is, in effect, to condone that sin, as well as to allow resentment to build within yourself at being used. Before confronting the manipulator, you need discernment from the Lord as to what the real sin is. Then, as difficult as it may be, you need to explain to the offender as unemotionally as possible that this behavior is unacceptable both before God and before you and that it must change, showing him the way to do this.

The epileptic man who stayed with us had learned deep patterns of manipulation and had left a trail of broken relationships, including his estranged wife and virtually every member of his family. Soon after he came to us, the old patterns were resumed. David found himself growing more and more angry as this man attempted to manipulate us and others in our church body. In response, David began to move toward the role of dictator. However, after he repented of his anger, he started to ask God to help him speak the truth in love as objectively as possible.

Needing a ride to a nearby city, the young man had asked one of our church friends for early-morning transportation. David awakened him that morning so that the fellow would be ready, then found himself again growing increasingly angry when the man was still in bed twenty minutes later. Instead of spluttering at him, which would have enabled him to think that anger was one of David's problems, David knocked on the door and calmly said, "You asked John to come out of his way to pick you up. If you aren't up and ready on time, you are being very selfish and inconsiderate of him." His response was a positive one, freeing David from the churning inside.[2]

Establishing Terms and Bounds

One of the best ways to handle manipulation is to be sure that each person involved in an extended family ministry clearly understands the bounds and terms of living conditions. This may seem at first dictatorial or harsh, but imagine yourself going into a new situation. If no bounds are given, you find yourself groping and stumbling, not sure of what is expected.

Living Terms

Most extended families interviewed saw the same basic living terms:

1. The person must be in school or work at a job.
2. He must take care of his physical body.
3. He must attend at least the worship service of the local church.

1. The need for work or study: Boredom often comes from idleness, which, as Isaac Watts reminds us, leads to the mischief Satan finds for idle hands to do. The scriptural injunction given to the Thessalonians was "if a man will not

2. David Augsburger has written an excellent manual on handling manipulation, *Caring Enough to Confront*, revised (Glendale, Calif: Regal Books, 1980).

work, he shall not eat" (II Thess. 3:12b). Even in a time of high unemployment, jobs in nursing homes or as security guards seem to be available.

Since the goal is for the individual to become independent, he must find a way to earn a living. He must contribute financially to help carry his weight in your family and begin to learn to budget his funds. Here, though, the newcomer probably needs support and encouragement as he seeks employment. Past failures may haunt him, and he may need restructuring even in setting up a time schedule to ensure that he will arrive at his job promptly and has the energy to perform his tasks. You must continually reward him verbally as he achieves this restructuring in his life.

A lack of self-respect may be one of the greatest problems your newcomer faces. Work, if handled properly, can be an important tool for re-creating his self-respect. For some, working on necessary tasks around the house is the beginning. It is important for such a person to see results; so you might structure his first responsibilities around the home to accomplish this. Most of the time you will need to help him assemble the right tools and give careful instruction, but not in a condescending way.

In having an individual work around your home, you must also realize that the job may not be done as efficiently or as effectively as you wish. One teenager who stayed with us was sent to the woods behind our house to cut six beanpoles for our garden. David walked back to the wooded area with him, brought the right tools, helped him cut the first sapling, and left him there. An hour and a half later the boy emerged from the woods exhausted after cutting two more poles. Yet, because he had deep mental problems, which left him with a constantly clouded mind, to finish even part of a job unsupervised was a feat.

If the young person is school-age, he certainly must attend classes. We have found, as have many other extended families, that school officials are cooperative in offering resources such as testing and counseling. For some children, placement in a school more conducive to their learning needs is the answer, and most states have an evaluation procedure that can find the right setting for them. The Sheptocks of Peapack, New Jersey, who have opened their home to many handicapped and multi-handicapped children, have found that the schools have provided the right facilities for even their most difficult-to-place child. Ten-year-old Barbie, mentioned previously, attended a local Christian school, where her teacher worked closely with both the extended family parents and Barbie's natural parents. You, as the extended family parent, must be diligent in contacting the school, so that you can reinforce the child at home.

2. The care of the physical body: When a newcomer enters the O'Carroll family, his first purchase is his own pair of running shoes. As George O'Carroll puts it, "We've noticed that a lot of these people are quite sessile—they're content to sit around and do nothing. Even though it's hard on them at first, soon they get the circulation going and physiologically they're in better shape and we can begin to work with them."

Not all extended families use this approach, but all acknowledge that it is essential to care for the body God has given each of us. Providing balanced meals and diet, ensuring the proper amount of sleep, and creating opportunities for physical exercise all help bring the body into good shape. In rural areas, working in the garden or with farm animals accomplishes this. Others advocate more formal exercise. We are finding that the elimination of junk food from our house forces us to make better choices for our diet.

Before we began giving this area adequate attention,

some who stayed with us would stay up late watching television and be unable to function the next morning. One girl who, before staying with us, found it difficult to get up for school in the morning, no longer had that problem once she began to go to bed at a more reasonable time.

3. Attendance at the worship service of a local church body: Your involvement in this ministry has come as a response to the call of Jesus Christ. He is the Lord of your life. It is important that your newcomer, now a part of your family, be exposed to the truth and glory of your Lord as you gather with His people for worship.

John Vandegriff sees having a regular family devotional life as one qualification for those wishing to enter this ministry. More than a mere formality, that time serves as a reflection of the important place Christ possesses in your family.

While the degree of participation your new family member has in your church will obviously depend on his response to the gospel, he must agree, as part of your Christian family, to accompany you to worship or, if acceptable, to continue worshiping at his own church. Without this, your own family can be negatively affected by what amounts to a double standard.

Bounds

Along with terms that clarify basic responsibilities, it is only fair for the incoming family member to be aware of any bounds your family may have. Each family will set slightly different limits, depending on the makeup of your own natural family, the setup of your home, and the convictions of your heart.

1. Use of family possessions: When someone enters

your home, you want to make him feel at ease. Yet, when a manipulative personality comes through the door, the result may be that your possessions are no longer shared, but seized. The television, radio, and stereo seem special targets, and you may have to establish a basic policy governing their use.

The first guidelines are the ones you have established for your own family's viewing. (If you've given up your TV, skip this section and rejoice that you have one less problem to face!) We are very careful about what is seen on our TV, watching mainly the news, a few sports, and some educational children's programs. If we were to violate our standards and allow a newcomer to watch shows we find harmful, we would only add confusion in the minds of our two preschoolers. We have refused requests for such shows and explained our reasons for doing so, without feeling the need to make accommodations.

If the TV has no restrictions, you may find your new family member curled in front of the set for hours, caring to do little else. One young man who came for part of the summer brought his own set with him. We were caught by surprise and told him it had to be off by 11 p.m. Since we are in bed by ten most nights, we were not there to check that he followed our instructions. The next morning, though, when David tried to awaken him for work, it was obvious he had stayed up much later. We had to confront him on this and have him see the consequence of his action. Another man began to sneak upstairs after we had retired for the night, bringing the TV to his room and remaining up most of the night.

The stereo and the radio present other problems. Hibernation may set in as the newcomer retires to his room accompanied by headphones. Some families deal with this by eliminating radios and stereos outright. Others help the individual toward maturity by having him plan his time, so that he can find the right balance between relaxation and work. The volume level of a stereo or radio can become another bone of contention. A good leverage for control is the loss of listening privileges if the volume gets too high. Another family informed their newcomer he had to hear the first call for dinner, or he would go hungry. The stereo volume lowered immediately!

Whatever policy you adopt, you must provide alternatives to listening and watching. Reading a good book is one substitute. Another is working on a craft project or a building project. Playing games or engaging in another recreation is a third. Going out for a fun night is yet another. Finding a person's interests and helping him develop new ones can help replace old habits that lead to laziness.

2. Kitchen privileges: Ruth, in the process of opening our home to others, has had a battle with our refrigerator. She usually shops once at the beginning of the week and then is dismayed by Wednesday when she sees how quickly the shelves are being emptied. We are called to be stewards, but not hoarders, and so this is an area that needs consideration.

Most newcomers are, at first, cautious about roaming through the available foodstuffs; so this may not be a great problem. Serving three well-balanced meals with plenty of food is also a preventive measure for misuse of the kitchen. Identifying certain items as snack foods is another device that helps eliminate finding Friday's supper eaten Tuesday afternoon. Some families, however, do declare the kitchen "off base" until they are convinced the new family member can be trusted.

This becomes again an individual choice for your family. We don't make an issue over it. But if there is abuse, David (since Ruth is still struggling with being objective about this) usually explains that we need a certain food item for supper. We have found overall that God does supply our food needs more than adequately. Yet it may be necessary, if you acquire a foodaholic, to establish policies for kitchen use.

3. Use of the telephone: Mr. Bell's invention can be a tool for good or evil. You should then be aware of its potential and set some ground rules for its use.

Two fellows we had staying with us at different times demonstrated this to us. One young man, mentioned previously, had serious psychological problems. He was competing with his father for the mother's time, attention, and affection. Soon after he arrived, he began to use the phone to call home, all with the purpose of intimidating his mother. We were unaware of this problem and thought he was merely checking on his family. When his mother told us of the situation—as she should have when he entered our home, since this was a long-standing problem—we could begin to help him use the phone more constructively. The other man would call friends, old and new, sharing his past problems in order to get sympathy. This conflicted with what we were trying to teach him—the need to work in the present and for the future and take responsibility for his actions.

Keep an account of phone calls made, since the bill quickly mounts up. We use a small pad near the phone for this purpose. Some families limit their newcomer to two five-minute calls per night, until he has shown responsibility in this or another area. Other families require the new member to receive permission before making any out-of-area call.

4. Drinking, drugs, smoking: Whatever is illegal has no place in the extended family. Therefore, the use of drugs or drinking by a minor is automatically taboo. That does not mean, though, that a problem with the abuse of drugs and alcohol will not come.

You should become familiar with the variety of drugs and their effects. Most of us are uninformed in this area. Schools often give drug awareness programs for parents, and the local library has other resources. If a person entering your home has a serious drug problem, perhaps you should refer him to a center that specializes in this area.

Many extended families deal with the problem of alcohol by totally eliminating it from the home. Others opt for moderation, but always with control.

Smoking can be another problem. Some families again outlaw this practice altogether. Others show the newcomer how addiction to this habit is a waste of his money, body, and time.

It is not always possible, in our estimation, to establish a no-smoking policy without turning a person away. Adherence to such a policy is not essential to enter the kingdom of heaven. You might instead focus on helping the smoker set goals toward quitting and give him support toward that aim.

We live in a flammable, one-hundred-year-old barn. Because of the fire hazard and our personal health requirements, we confine smoking to the outdoors. This is habit-limiting, since smoking becomes an inconvenience, especially in the winter or on rainy nights. A compromise such as this may keep you from focusing on secondary issues, and yet give you freedom from concern about fire and the discomfort of the smoke itself.

5. Private space for your newcomer: As you show radical hospitality, part of your goal is to help your new family member feel at home. Here you may have to set some bounds for yourself. Each person, including your newcomer, needs some territory and time to call his own. Setting aside a place he knows is his alone, however small, will help him see that you have respect for him as a fellow human made in God's image. Scheduling some "alone time" is important in teaching him the need for quiet and reflection and will give you as extended family hosts your necessary private time, too. If he becomes highly secretive, of course, you will have to confront him, but always without robbing him of the dignity that accompanies being God's highest creation, fallen though each of us is.

When in Doubt, Write It Out!

Whatever God leads you to establish as terms of living and bounds, writing these down is a vital step. This gives you an objective basis for confrontation when it is necessary, for the terms have been agreed upon beforehand.

The following is a contract we set up, rather belatedly, for the epileptic man who was staying with us:

REQUIREMENTS FOR STAYING AT BERACHAH BARN

1. A weekly schedule must be developed, approved by Dave or Ruth, and followed unless permission is given otherwise.

   The schedule must include:
   a. meal times (three balanced meals a day)
   b. eight hours of sleep
   c. work hours
   d. three hours of cleaning at the Barn

2. Starting January 1, $25 a week will be required for room and board.

3. All phone calls will be paid up before additional calls can be made.

4. By March 1, 1980, a room must be found and independence established.

Coming to terms is of utmost priority. Lest this seem harsh and dictatorial, it must be noted that the contract must be drawn up with input from the new family member as well. That is why it is important for him to decide on his goals in this relationship. From these goals, terms and bounds can be mutually established.

Family Meetings

By now, you should be able to see how important communication is in this ministry. To facilitate such openness, many extended families have what can be termed family meetings. At these sessions new policies can be discussed, problems can be aired, suggestions can be made, and, above all, prayer can be shared.

Some families choose to have weekly formal meetings. The Haft has one supper meal for all the community members, followed by a session where problems that have arisen during the week can be handled. A formal meeting allows you to view the varying perspectives on a difficult situation. It is also the best choice for those beginning to deal in radical hospitality, since it provides a built-in structure for confrontation.

Others choose to keep their meetings less formal, participating instead in discussions around the dinner table. The O'Carrolls find this method suits their busy lifestyle, in which family members scatter most evenings. At dinner time, the O'Carrolls feel they best help the newcomer become integrated into the family as all participate in sharing events of the day and joking with one another.

Another approach is to have a meeting only when the need arises. The Vandegriffs have gravitated toward this method, having found regularly scheduled meetings no longer necessary.

Whatever approach you choose, it is paramount to have a time to interact with each other. It is far too easy to say you do not have time for this and, instead, internalize your frustrations, only to explode later.

Learning from Failure

Most extended families could publish a book on their failures. The ratio of success to failure in this ministry is small. We are earthen vessels working with earthen vessels.

The first time failure comes it can be devastating. You might feel angry that you were manipulated, used, unappreciated. You might cry. You might become withdrawn and despondent. You might tend to see the one who rejected your help as having no redeeming qualities whatsoever.

Your new family member has one of two responses to the terms and bounds you, with him, have defined and agreed on: submissive obedience or defiant rebellion. Since change is difficult, rebellion is often the choice. In such a case you must commit the person to God, trusting Him to use someone else to water what you have planted.

It may be that your newcomer resented that your family *does* work well together. The contrast between his former lifestyle and the one he saw in your home may have been too glaring. Perhaps, because your family was attempting to live by biblical principles, he could not blame others for his own faults; and rather than repent and find forgiveness, he chose to run.

Jon and Cheryl Heymann, a pastor and wife from Clinton Corners, New York, had opened their home to a 22-year-old man who had literally been living on the streets for the previous ten years. His mother had deserted the family when he was seven, and his father had died five years later. The time came, though, when the Heymanns also had to ask Doug to leave their home because he would not submit to their authority. Within four days Doug ended up in the county jail and a few months later was sent to a federal penitentiary. When he completed his sentence, however, he returned to the Heymanns, where he settled in and is now on his own, holding a job. The hope of the gospel that changes lives has been clearly demonstrated.

At other times you may have been too harsh and not as understanding as you should have been. In that case, you must come before God, repent, and accept His forgiveness, trusting Him to redeem what you may have destroyed. Scripture also calls for you to go to the person you have wronged, seeking his forgiveness.

Another step in learning from failure is to discuss it with your family. Talk of ways of preventing the same mistakes from happening again. Brainstorm for more productive ways of dealing with similar circumstances.

We learned much from failure when our epileptic man decided we were using him, and he would no longer let himself be stepped on. After a month of irresponsible behavior on his part, not taking his medication, and abusing his health, he was hospitalized with an infection. When he returned, we gave him only a little sympathy, since more would have encouraged him to do little for himself. We insisted he would have to find work or, if he were really disabled, apply for public assistance. He then became angry and lashed out at us for not understanding him.

We had to deal with his accusations. He was a repulsive

person in many ways, and it was difficult to love him. Yet, this was one of his manipulative techniques to make us feel guilty. After we had examined ourselves, we were able to confront him and not allow him to project his own sin onto us.

At our family meeting the day after he left, we explored our failure. We learned first that we had to establish terms from the beginning. We also had to determine whether we could effectively minister to anyone who wanted to come, or if we were better referring such a person elsewhere. We repented of our failure to act, at times, in love, yet we rejoiced in what we had gained through the experience.

The feelings we have shared are echoed by others in the extended family ministry. It is good to know that God is sovereign and will accomplish His purposes.

God will take what you learn from your first and your ensuing failures and enable you to die to self, to change circumstances in your home for the better, and to prepare for the next person sent your way. Failure can be God's tool to chip away at us, conforming us to the image of His Son.

Conclusion

The wounds of those who need radical hospitality are deep. Radical surgery is often the only treatment that can bring life. In an extended family, the surgery that creates change is often painful and met with resistance. The anesthesia of clearly spelling out terms and bounds and the excising of manipulation by loving confrontation must be done. And if surgery fails or the patient refuses to continue treatment, the host family must evaluate and, in some cases, repent, hoping and seeking God to accomplish His purposes by other means.

Activities

1. Brainstorm on ways a newcomer might use manipulation as he enters your home. How might you be tempted to use manipulation in return? What are some alternatives to manipulation?

2. How do basic living terms advocated in this chapter—need for work or study, care of the physical body, attendance at the worship service of a local church body—reflect a scriptural focus on the whole man?

3. As husband and wife, discuss the areas under setting bounds—use of family possessions; kitchen privileges; use of the telephone; drinking, drugs, and smoking; privacy. What restrictions do you advocate in each area? In what areas would you find it easy to enforce your restrictions? In which ones would you have difficulty?

4. Why would a family meeting be a good vehicle for confrontation? When would a one-to-one confrontation be better used?

CHAPTER TEN

The Local Church—
The Place for Help

The apostle Paul remarked to the church at Corinth: "There is no need for me to write to you about this service to the saints. For I know your eagerness to help and I have been boasting about it . . ." (II Cor. 9:1-2a). Unfortunately, many churches today could not be the recipients of that letter, for they know little of bearing one another's burdens or lifting the load to make it more tolerable. Others, however, because they have seen this lack, are making the effort to grow in learning what it means to refresh the hearts of the saints, as Philemon had.

In the extended family ministry, you must not be afraid to seek help from fellow Christians. Indeed, to seek help is a must in our thinking, which is why we have emphasized that the extended family should be associated with and under the care of a local church. Through your involvement in the extended family, you can provide the opportunity, as Paul said to Timothy, for others to grow in washing the feet of the saints.

102

Initially, some congregations and church leaders may be suspicious of the radical hospitality you are offering outsiders. They may see the risks involved and fear the consequences that may befall your own family. If this is the case, your first goal must be educating the brethren, showing them that the Scripture does make us responsible to show hospitality toward the alien and the stranger.

This education can be accomplished in several ways. On an individual basis, you may share books that emphasize the need for Christian community. You may then ask your reader to consider prayerfully the implications of his reading. Talk informally with friends about your concerns in this area. Invite your church elders or pastor to examine with you the biblical basis for radical hospitality as seen in the first part of this book. Reading the entire book itself may be the means of allaying fears that you are forming a commune or cult.

In other congregations, the pastor himself has led the way in establishing credibility for the extended family ministry. In our interviewing, we found many such men whose families saw the need to take the battered, bruised, and broken into their homes. In turn, the church witnessed the impact made on the newcomers' lives, and others in the congregation were willing to open their homes as well.

Most of us are innately fearful of change or new ideas. Therefore, any education that takes place must be done tactfully and prayerfully. In the case of our own church, we found that our people first needed to learn to be open with each other before we were ready to be hospitable in this more radical way. Taking time to educate, confront, and reassure may prevent any later misunderstandings.

What part then should your church leaders and congregation play in the extended family ministry? Three areas immediately come to mind: they can support you in prayer, they can give you physical relief, and they can supplement your resources.

Prayer for Decision Making and Encouragement

The demands of an extended family ministry will force you to pray. We have personally grown in our prayer life as we have seen the need to request protection for our children and our home, wisdom in dealing with difficult people, victory over anger and hurt, and correction of our own faults. As Paul requests the saints to be praying for him in his imprisonment, so you will want others in your church to be remembering you. Having a few close friends in a prayer chain can give the renewal and confidence to press on when you feel like quitting.

When Kathy, the teenager from our church, came to stay with us, we had the prayer support of the entire body. The women's Bible study gave this high priority. The prayer chain was ready at all times. God honored this working together and brought healing in the relationship, even through the strain of the discovery that Kathy's mother had rapidly spreading bone cancer. As we ministered to Kathy, we did so with much confidence from God, a result of the prayers of the saints.

You will also want to use your church elders as a sounding board for making decisions. We recommend that you seek their approval as you embark on this ministry. Ask them to pray for you and to be available for help in the decision-making processes, which are crucial at times. If the elders understand your ministry and are spiritual men, their decisions will be in line with God's will, and they will confirm your leadings time and again.

Other couples who are also involved in this extended

family ministry may be able to meet with you, praying together and offering their perspectives. One friend whose family was involved in this ministry in a remote setting felt this lack of counsel. The family has since left this ministry, attributing a sense of aloneness as part of their reason for doing so. They had, however, made little effort to associate themselves with the local body of believers who met a few miles away and who could have provided the needed direction and encouragement.

Part of the ministry of the body is to build up one another. Although God Himself gives us strong encouragement, as Hebrews 6:18 tells us, we often need to have encouragement come in tangible ways from others. Prayer and the decisions growing out of it will bring needed encouragement for the hard times in the extended family ministry. As your church continues in prayer for you, you will find God's grace overcoming your discouragement, enabling you to regain your perspective and grow in faith.

Getting Away to Recuperate

In times of discouragement in particular, but even in times of encouragement, radical hospitality has a draining effect physically, emotionally, and spiritually. The inner and outer man must be renewed. David finds a prayer walk in the woods or a day away as God's means of refreshing him. When he doesn't take the time for his personal renewal, he tends to view himself as a martyr and feels overburdened, all of which leads to isolation and discouragement.

The local church can help provide needed time for rest and recuperation by opening its homes to your new family member for a day or an evening. Some can offer jobs, providing work for your newcomer and a break for you. Others might invite him or her for dinner and a chance to get to know another family.

At the church in the Bronx of which Bob and Jeanne Hall are a part, four households have been set aside for extended family ministering, while the other households in the church provide relief for a day or an evening. This enables the ministering families to maintain time for their natural families and relieves the pressure and strain often present when a person with deep problems enters a home.

Sometimes the recuperation comes in the form of a meal brought to you. When we had our additional two family members arrive within a day of each other last winter, a young couple from church called to announce that they were bringing dinner. They wanted to be sure Ruth was not overburdened. We saw this as one of God's surprises that usually come when we are honest with one another. That morning Ruth, in her Bible study group, had shared our need for prayer support, and that same night a couple, neither of whom had been at the study or heard of the prayer request, met our physical need.

In another church, a "meal-a-month" program has been part of the answer to the needed break. Those not involved full-time with radical hospitality invite the new family member to their homes for dinner. This is carefully organized so that the newcomer is not singled out as a burden or bother. But it does allow the ministering family to have dinner alone and, as one interviewee stated, "Usually out!"

Ministering to one person at a time does have practical advantages over ministering to a large group. It is usually easier to find a place to go for an evening or day for one individual than it is for eight. It can become so difficult and complex to arrange a replacement when you are ministering to a large family, that you end up resigning yourself to remaining home and not getting the needed rest. The "burn out" rate among those who have large extended families is often high because of this very factor.

Resources from the Body

Another advantage of working closely with your local church is the availability of resources it offers. Your time and skills are limited. As your church practices meeting the needs of the saints, you soon may discover some who can provide for what you lack.

One area in which the church may prove to be resourceful is in locating jobs. A teenager coming into your home may find day work in the homes of the congregation, thus providing an income for him and relief for you. Working around the church itself, doing odd jobs, provides another type of outlet for the new family member. Others may know the job market well enough to give you direction. You also might have a Christian businessman whose ministry could be to work with your newcomer, patiently teaching him skills and supervising him. Keep a list of those who might be able to help in this way.

To combat boredom and to establish habits of productivity, it is, as previously mentioned, important to find an interest for your incoming family member. Here again the church body can be of service. You may not have the tools or skills needed to pursue his interest. An amateur photographer might instruct him in darkroom techniques, sharing a skill and building a relationship. A competent seamstress might help your new teenager alter a pair of pants. Your new family member will then be better able to understand that your times of worship together as a church body prepare you to live out the gospel each day.

Conclusion

The apostle John instructs in I John 4:18, "Dear children, let us not love with words or tongue, but with actions and in truth." Radical hospitality calls the entire church to this "action love" as the body becomes involved in sharing in your ministry. As you seek help from your fellow members, you may be the catalyst for renewing this love among yourselves as people begin to minister and care in this practical way. If you instead attempt to "go it alone," you only court disaster, since in God's design none of us has been given all spiritual gifts or all physical means. We all must depend on others in the body so that we may all reach "unity in the faith and in the knowledge of the Son of God and become mature, attaining to the whole measure of the fullness of Christ" (Eph. 4:13).

Activities

1. One of your closest friends in church decides to open his home in radical hospitality. List four practical ways that you personally could be of help.

2. Compile a list of resources available among your local church members for providing jobs and sharing skills. Keep this list on file and update it periodically.

CHAPTER ELEVEN

Pray Without Ceasing—
And You Will Pray!

Paul writes to the church at Ephesus:

> For this reason, ever since I heard about your faith in the
> Lord Jesus and your love for all the saints, I have not
> stopped giving thanks for you, remembering you in my
> prayers. I keep asking that the God of our Lord Jesus
> Christ, the glorious Father, may give you a Spirit of
> wisdom and revelation, so that you might know Him
> better. I pray also that the eyes of your heart may be
> enlightened in order that you may know the hope to
> which He has called you, the riches of His glorious
> inheritance in the saints, and His incomparably great
> power for us who believe (Eph. 1:15-19).

What marvelous and necessary requests Paul makes on
their behalf. Then at the end of the same Epistle, he also
instructs the Ephesian Christians, in turn, to pray for him
and even for themselves:

And pray in the Spirit on all occasions with all kinds of prayers and requests. With this mind, be alert and always keep on praying for all the saints (Eph. 6:18).

The extended family ministry is one that depends on prayer —not only the prayers of the saints in your local church body, but your own personal time spent before God.

The words of one man we interviewed were echoed by every other Christian who exercised radical hospitality: "Not a morning goes by that I don't find myself asking for God's strength and wisdom as I begin the day." How, then, does prayer affect the extended family?

Dealing with Anger

One of the first reasons to pray is to help you control anger. A newcomer's irresponsibility and manipulation may readily trigger anger within you. Prayer returns you to a proper frame of mind. It enables you to die to self, to put off anger which might never have surfaced had this person not entered your home. Prayer reminds you that your life is not your own and alerts you that what was broken, stolen, or misused may have begun to control you. You can choose to love in spite of the hurt. Prayer then leads you to creative solutions for confronting and controlling the faulty behavior, giving you the right restrictions, the right words, and the right motives for the confrontation. While, in anger, your initial reaction may be to tell the newcomer to pack his bags and get out, prayer gives you a calmness and objectivity to accomplish God's purpose of making men whole.

Praying for Protection

We pray for the protection of our home and especially our children. The effect this ministry can have on children is one of the reasons some families leave such an outreach, for children can become negatively affected and themselves rebel. If you fail with your own children in order to succeed with the new family member, you in reality totally fail! A newcomer may eventually have to leave your home if he is a detriment to your children, but this decision must be reached after prayerful reflection on biblical priorities.

One couple whom we interviewed experienced God's protection in a clear way when a disturbed young man who had come to live with them attempted to set the house on fire. The wife returned just at the right moment, before the damage became too extensive. They are convinced that God had heard their many prayers for His protection and intervened with His timing.

Praying for Love

Christians are called to minister love, love that is not based in emotion or feeling, but that finds its foundation in seeking the highest good for any fellow human created in the image of God. The *agape* love, as the Greek terms it, is not an involuntary response, but is rather a willful obedience to God's command to love even our enemies.

Agape love is something we all fall short of implementing on an ongoing basis. No one, except God Himself, is full of good will in words, deeds, and thoughts toward others at all times. But, as Romans 5:5 states, "God has poured out His love into our hearts by the Holy Spirit, whom He has given us." Praying with your partner can be a great source of help and comfort as you reach out to God for this love.

Ruth had become quite discouraged with a man who had practically taken over our home before we realized it. We had been granted a temporary respite while he had been hospitalized for a week, but the next day he was scheduled to be released and would return to us. As we prayed together that night, Ruth could summon none of the love of God to help her minister. David prayed that we might look beyond his faults and see his need, a prayer God used to speak to Ruth and give her the love she needed. When our young man came in the next morning, Ruth was able to say, "Welcome home!" with a smile and conviction.

Praying for the Outreach of the Gospel

You may feel like the servant in the parable who starts early, works a full day, yet receives the same wage as the one who worked only one-fourth of the day. A high percentage of those who come to stay with you may not enter the kingdom of God during their stay there. Most of those who come through your door will have complex problems stemming from their own and their parents' sin and rebellion. Many years of intensive work may be necessary before they can respond to the good news of salvation. You may be planting seeds that will have their increase years later. Yet, since God is not willing that any should perish, you will be praying for them, for the unveiling of their minds, which have been blinded by Satan, and for the tenderizing of their hearts by God's love.

Evangelism through the extended family ministry must be, as must any such efforts to share the gospel, surrounded by prayer, on the part of the host family and your church body, that "God may open a door for our message."

Paul wrote those words, urging the Colossians to pray, "so that we may proclaim the mystery of Christ" (Col. 4:3). The open door in the extended family ministry is, in effect, your new family member's willingness to submit to authority.

When structure and discipline exercised in the context of love are brought into the life of one who formerly had neither, one of two directions is pursued, as noted earlier. Your newcomer may run from these impositions, rebels and leave your family or force you to ask him to leave because of continued defiance, or he may submit to the loving authority you have offered. This willingness to submit to authority becomes the key attitude needed for evangelism to occur. Once he submits to God's authority as found in your home, he may very well submit to God's authority in his life as you lead him step by step to acknowledge the lordship of Christ and his need of repentance and faith as a response to God's love.

Sheryl and Donna are examples of those who came into God's kingdom through the witness of the extended family. Sheryl spent much of her time with her neighbors down the street, people who had welcomed many to live in their home. She accepted Christ as Savior and eventually became part of that family when her own family life crumbled. Donna came to meet her extended family when her brother brought her to a Bible study at their home. She did not at that time see her need of Christ, but after she had moved in with the family because she dropped out of school and needed some stability, she came to realize that Jesus Christ was the only one who could integrate her life.

Pray as well for the salvation of the natural parents of the child with whom you are working. If the goal is to bring the whole family back together, then God needs to be working in each life to bring each one to Him.

Without Ceasing

Prayer is the life-breath of the extended family: praying alone, with your partner, and the entire family, including your new member. But just as breathing depends on actual inhaling and exhaling and not on a detailed knowledge of the breathing mechanisms involved in respiration, so, in radical hospitality, knowledge of how prayer affects this ministry is insufficient unless it is actually fleshed out in daily participation.

Scripture abounds with many instances of personal prayer. The Psalms teach us adoration, thanksgiving, confession, petition, and intercession. Taking time daily alone with God is the necessary foundation for effectiveness in any ministry. Whether it is time spent in a quiet corner in your room in the morning or evening or a prayer walk such as David finds necessary, personal prayer is a must. Paul, in Colossians 4:2, says to the Christians at Colosse, "devote yourselves to prayer, being watchful and thankful." God will work uniquely through prayer as you acknowledge your dependence on Him, making ministry possible and successful.

Praying as a couple is also an important part of your ministry. Often you may be the means of ministering God's grace to your partner, who has been disheartened, angered, or deeply hurt by your new family member. We have found this to be especially effective in our relationship as we pray for each other. By praying together, we are also able to hold each other accountable for what each has said before the Lord. Then if one of us chooses to go against God's way, the other can lovingly confront and point the way back to repentance and forgiveness.

As a couple you will also pray together for wisdom and direction. James 1:5 promises to fill the lacks you will have in this area as you are faced with many complex situations. Partner praying in our home often occurs when a crisis arises. We have learned that it is impossible to find solutions without this time together. Without prayer, we are tempted to act on our immediate reactions, which are often emotional responses. When one teenager who came to us began to stay out late and ignore our restrictions, David's angry reaction was to pack up his belongings, leave them outside, and tell him to stay out with them. As we prayed together, he found God's peace dissipating his anger. The next day David was able to confront him and discipline him in a calm way, which enabled him to realize he was responsible for the consequences of his defiance, rather than to shift blame onto David's anger.

Praying as a family also gives the vitality needed in radical hospitality. Your own children and your new family member will see the importance that talking with God has in your own life, and they will be able to worship and respond as they see God answering His children's requests.

For us, praying at mealtimes provides our family the opportunity to talk to God together. Rather than simply being thankful for our food, we express our thanks toward God for who He is or what He has done for us during that day and make requests for others as an expression of our love and concern. Others have set time each evening for the family to pray together. Some, as they pray for friends and missionaries, keep a family scrapbook with pictures and relevant information. As your family prays together, your newcomer will see how God is concerned for your daily needs and the needs of others, and he may come to see that God is also concerned for him.

While praying *about* your new family member is foundational for your ministry with him, praying *with* him and *teaching* him to pray are two of the blocks to be placed upon that foundation. In prayer, you may be able to confront your newcomer in an easier way as you bring his needs before God, acknowledging that God alone can bring the necessary changes.

Just as Philippians 4:6 admonishes us to present all needs before the Lord, you will find yourself praying with your new family member when he goes for a job, and together praising God when this prayer is answered. You will teach him, as I John 1:9 states, to come before God in repentance when there is sin. After failure, you will pray together for consolation to try again, remembering Paul's words in II Corinthians 12:9. After confrontation, together you can ask for God's strength to do what is right, knowing the promise of Philippians 4:13. As you pray together, showing him through Scripture why you are doing so, he will be able to see the reality of God's care and love and the enactment of God's grace.

For many who come into a place of radical hospitality, public prayer, even among two or three, may be foreign. Yet, as you show by example and God's Word that all believers can approach the Almighty through Jesus Christ, your new family member may, in the silence of his own room or heart, begin to express faith and thankfully make his petitions known to a God who cares and responds.

Conclusion

When the disciples asked Jesus to teach them to pray, He responded that they should pray in this way:

Our Father in heaven,
hallowed be your name;
your kingdom come,
your will be done on earth as it is in heaven.

Give us today our daily bread.
Forgive us our debts as we also have forgiven our debtors;
And lead us not into temptation,
but deliver us from the evil one (Matt. 6:9-13).

The Lord's prayer, as a model for all Christians, is especially appropriate as you engage in radical hospitality. Your relationship with your heavenly Father makes it possible for you to offer His care and hospitality to others whom He invites to be sons and daughters. His holiness gives you a measuring standard as you point your newcomer to salvation. You are involved in furthering God's kingdom and doing His will as the alien and stranger are brought into your home. You will see Him supply your daily needs and forgive you, as you, in turn, forgive those who will be in your debt. You will trust Him, in turn, to deliver you from the evil one. And you will see God receive the glory and the power as His purposes are accomplished.

A prayer that should also be on your lips daily, as you open your home to others, is Paul's prayer in Philippians 1:9-11, expressing the goal toward which you labor:

And this is my prayer: that your love may abound more and more in knowledge and depth of insight, so that you will be able to discern what is the best and may be pure and blameless until the day of Christ, filled with the fruit of righteousness that comes through Jesus Christ—to the glory and praise of God.

Activities

1. If you presently do not have family prayer time and devotions, determine as a family the best time and place for your family to do this. Then begin!

2. If you do have family prayer time and devotions, evaluate their effectiveness for each family member and brainstorm ways of improving them.

3. Check your local Christian bookstore for short books and pamphlets that would effectively communicate the way of salvation to a new family member.